Sports
from
HELL

For Geno, the Rolls-Royce of buddies

Also by Rick Reilly

Sports
from
HELL

■ ■ ■

My Search for the World's Dumbest Competition

Rick Reilly

DOUBLEDAY / ESPN BOOKS

DOUBLEDAY

Copyright © 2010 by Rick Reilly

All rights reserved. Published in the United States by Doubleday,
a division of Random House, Inc., New York, and in Canada
by Random House of Canada Limited, Toronto.
www.doubleday.com

DOUBLEDAY and the DD colophon are registered
trademarks of Random House, Inc.

The ESPN name and logo are registered
trademarks of ESPN, Inc.

Grateful acknowledgment is made to the following for permission
to reproduce their photographs:
Cover art and Chapter 2: Meagan J. Rhoten
Chapter 4: Rana Weaver, EMRTC/NMT
Chapter 13: Stefano Pasini/FOTO UP AGENCY
All other photos are courtesy of Cynthia Reilly, aka "TLC"

Library of Congress Cataloging-in-Publication Data
Reilly, Rick.
Sports from hell : my search for the world's dumbest
competition / Rick Reilly.
p.   cm.
1. Sports—Miscellanea.   I. Title.
GV707.R46 2009
796—dc22   2009025112

ISBN 978-0-385-51438-5

PRINTED IN THE UNITED STATES OF AMERICA

1 3 5 7 9 10 8 6 4 2

First Edition

You can sum up this sport in two words: You never know.

—Lou Duva, boxing trainer

Contents

Acknowledgments

It takes a lot of smart people to let a dumb guy write a whole book about stupid sports. For instance, how could I have experienced the utter exhaustion of playing a three-mile golf hole straight down a mountain full of explosives without the help of Ryan Klassen and Joel Haley? How would I have entered the world of illegal Jarts throwing without the aid of Jeff Balta? How would I have risked my walnuts in ferret legging without the three women at the Richmond Ferret Rescue League—Rita Jackson, Marlene Blackman, and Meagan J. Rhoten? (Please write me back, Spazz.) Without Kat Byles, I wouldn't have had a clue about how to cover a homeless soccer game. Without Ossi Arvela, I'd have had a stroke trying to figure out how to compete in the World Sauna Championships. Without a hand from Graham Walker, I'd have been stumped at the World Rock Paper Scissors Championships. I shudder to think what would have happened to me at Angola State Penitentiary without Angie Norwood, Gary Young, and Warden Burl Cain. Or Jody Taylor of the (now squashed) SoCal Scorpions women's pro football team. (Yes, Jody, the doctors think some of my vertebrae will grow back.) Thanks, too, to Danitra Alomia at the World Beer Pong Championships. Hope you get that Budweiser smell out of your hair. And cheers to London's Tim Woolgar, who not only explained chess boxing to me (it took hours), but then starred in it. And thanks to the best agent a man could have, Janet Pawson of Headline Media in New York, her trusty sidekick Michelle (Wood) Hall, Bill (Liam's Dad) Thomas at Doubleday, who went along with the madness, and Melissa Danaczko, who had to make sense of it all. Lastly, warehouses full of thanks go to the gorgeous and patient and ingenious researcher/organizer/travel agent TLC (The Lovely Cynthia), who made the idea of traipsing all around the world looking for stupidity seem like a brilliant idea.

Sports from HELL

Introduction: The Rules

Sportswriting can be about as tough as fur boxers. I've spooned the strawberries and cream at Wimbledon, slurped the mint juleps at the Kentucky Derby, sneezed into the azaleas at the Masters. I've sat on leather pressroom couches in front of glorious big screens from Dubai to Del Mar while pages of athletes' quotes were hand-delivered to me. I've been court-side at the Final Four and on the field for the Super Bowl and nearly had Mary Lou Retton land her famous 10s at the 1984 Olympics on my foot. I've covered all the sports everybody aches to attend.

Do you know how BORING that gets?

After thirty-one years of covering crap like that, I wanted to try covering some sports that were completely new, totally obscure, and mind-warpingly . . . dumb. The dumber, the better. I wanted to see if I could search the planet and find the single stupidest idea for sporting competition the world had ever devised. The thrill of victory, the forehead slap of "Why do you people DO this?" My motto was: If your sport is really moronic and witless, I'm the guy to write about it.

So, accompanied by my curvy girlfriend, Cynthia Puchniarz—aka TLC (The Lovely Cynthia)—a former Glendale, California, high school teacher, former Miss Teen California, and current research wizard, I set out in January of 2006 to do it. But first, over many, many tequilas, we decided on some ground rules:

1. It had to be an actual sport. Meaning: It had to be something people actually tried to win, something people cared about it, something open to anybody. There are dozens of Try to Fly Off the End of the Pier contests, bagsful of Who Can Come Up with the Dumbest Craft to Sail the Dry River regattas. Pah! It had to be dumb to everybody but those who played it. In fact, our rule of thumb was: If you would get punched if you told a guy his sport was stupid, it qualified.

2. It couldn't be stupid for the sake of being stupid. For instance, the World Shin Kicking Championships, which involves two combatants, their hands on each other's shoulders, kicking each other very hard in the shins. Seemed to have real stupidity potential. But then we saw this quote, from a shin-kicking official, who was trying to get shin kicking into the 2012 Olympics: "There's no need for dope tests—if anything, stupidity is encouraged." That nixed it. You can't KNOW your sport is stupid.

3. It couldn't exist mainly as tourist bait. It couldn't scream out, "Yes, this is a dumb sport and that's why the boys in marketing invented it, so YOU would come and spend all your euros!" The British are just awful about this. Take bog snorkeling, in which one dives into a disgusting muck-filled trench and swims 120 yards, with the proviso that one can't pull one's head out of the water. Besides, when one does come out, one finds one still in Mid Wales, so one just keeps swimming. Or cheese rolling, which involves letting a giant Double Gloucester cheese wheel roll down a hill, triggering a hundred or so drunk twenty-two-year-olds—falling ass-over-Guinness—in an attempt to be the first one across the line after it. In 2008, eighteen of the fifty contestants were injured.

You know what I say?

Good.

2

4. We had to actually watch people do it. There have been some wonderfully spackle-brained sports that no longer exist. Take the World Housekeeping Championships, for instance. Held at the Opryland Hotel, it was started in the 1970s by seventeen hotels in the Nashville area to promote pride in maid service. The maids fought to the last mint to see who could win titles in: Blindfolded Bed Making, Pillow Stuffing, and Slalom, which featured two-person teams pushing brooms to steer soaps and other amenities through an obstacle course of "wet floor" signs. How great is that? All that was missing was the Knocking Loudest at 6:07 A.M. While Ignoring the Do Not Disturb Sign competition.

5. It couldn't even be slightly famous. For instance, one sport I was dying to cover at first was noodling, which is the art of catching fish with your bare hands—the perfect solution for those fed up with the high cost of poles and worms. This was right up Dumb Drive. Noodlers have even been known to die doing it. We made plans to shadow a noodler—any noodler—in the big yearly noodling tournament in Oklahoma. The first guy we asked, a plumber, told TLC: "Nah, I'm hooked up with Discovery Channel this year." Then we tried a randomly toothed boat mechanic. "Sure," he said. "Hope you don't mind a crew from *National Geographic* along." The last guy—I think he was a professional drifter—spat out, "Sorry, I got a guy from *Time*." We decided to wait for the musical.

6. I didn't want to die covering it. This eliminated buzkashi, which is exactly like polo except instead of a small wooden ball you use the bloody corpse of a recently beheaded calf. Fun at parties! It's the national sport of Afghanistan. Teams of men on horseback using ropes try to drag a calf carcass—into which sand has been pounded—back to the winning circle while hundreds of other horsemen try to keep him from doing it, often with whips, for days at a time. Magnificently dumb. But I just couldn't see my kids having to tell people, "Dad died in Kabul when three buzkashists mistook him for a headless goat."

7. I couldn't have already covered it. For instance: lawn mower racing, which remains the only motor sport in the world where you can watch the pack go by, go get a bratwurst and a Pabst, and be back in time for the next pass. I liked it, though, if only for the names they give their rigs: "Sodzilla," "The Lawn Ranger," and "The Yankee Clipper." And I'd already investigated blimp racing, although there was only one blimp in the sky at the time, and that was the one I was driving: the Goodyear Blimp. If you ever want to do it, don't. They redline at fifteen miles per hour and there is no bathroom. Which is why if you happened to be at the Indianapolis Colts–Baltimore Ravens exhibition game a few years back, I'd like to apologize. Those were not summer showers.

8. It had to at least resemble a sport. This left out Extreme Ironing (which I did on the floor of the New York Stock Exchange anyway, just for the photo), the Air Guitar Championships, and Shotgun Golf, in which one advances a golf ball by means of a shotgun blast. That turned out to be entirely made up and passed off as real by the late Hunter S. Thompson. Hate to be a caddy for it.

Anyway, off we went. It would take us three and a half years, eight countries, and about 373 Red Roof Inns before our quest was complete. We found thirteen sports that we believe can out-stupid anything a committee of Dennis Rodman, John Daly, and Courtney Love could come up with. The things I did, the interviews I conducted, and the sentences I found myself writing actually reduced my IQ. So much so that after I finally turned the manuscript in, all I could think to say was: "How 'bout them Cowboys!"

1

World Sauna Championships

OK, kids, today's activity is to go down to your local Pizza Hut, have them set the oven for 261 degrees, and insert your entire body into it. The tips of your ears start to ignite. The backs of your arms scream. Your throat feels like somebody stuck a tiki torch down it. Your lips are bitten by large, unseen raccoons. You vow to move to Alaska. And you haven't even hit thirty seconds.

Now do it for ten minutes or more and you have an idea of what it's like to compete in quite possibly the world's dumbest sport—the World Sauna Championships.

I know. I entered.

. . .

These are the 9th Annual World Sauna Championships in Hei-nola, Finland, a Heidi-esque little lake-riddled town 140 kilo-meters north of Helsinki. I've covered a lot of thrilling athletic endeavors, but never men sitting in small rooms and sweating. What other championships does the world have? Napping? Barcalounging? Standing in Front of the Fridge?

Announcer: And now Struhdler leans in for the leftover tuna—nope! No! He switches to the fudge!

As we drove up, my mind reeled at what kind of things com-petitors in the World Sauna Championships say to sportswriters afterward in the locker room. "I just got hot. What can I say?"

I went over the rules. Simple. Competing in "six-person heats"—said without irony—the field of eighty-four men (including me) and eighteen women battle to see whose skin can boil last. You may wear only bathing suits that go eight inches down the leg and absolutely nothing else. (Women can wear one-piece bathing suits.) You can wipe sweat from your face, but not your body. You cannot cover your ears. You may not lean over too far. You get one warning, then you're out. Ambulances will be standing by. Good luck!

I wondered if sauna sitting has trash-talking like other sports. For instance, what if I came into my heat on the first day with a lit Winston and a cup of coffee? Maybe look at the other five guys and go, "Hey, when are they gonna turn this bitch on?" Start knocking on the window and yelling, "Let's get some heat in here! You want us to catch our deaths?" Maybe look at the crotch of the guy next to me and go, "That's weird. I thought COLD caused shrinkage." Or maybe wait outside the sauna while six *other* guys are about to go in and hand them a half-baked ziti. "Hey, would you mind tak-ing this in there? I've got a potluck in, like, twenty minutes."

In her research, TLC discovered that there was an Australian gambling site that has set the odds. Three-time defending champ Timmo (the Great) Kaukonen is a 2.15-to-1 favorite. I was listed at 101-to-1.

As if.

First of all, nobody but a Finn has ever won the World Sauna Championships. In fact, nobody but a Finn has ever been in the six-man finals. There are 5.2 million Finns and 3 million saunas. Legend has it most Finns are *born* in saunas. To a Finn, a sauna is a holy place. Then again, so is Hell.

Secondly, I wouldn't bet on me at 1,000,001 to one. At that point, I had saunaed five times in my life. I had about as much chance as a slice of Neopolitan ice cream. But the gambling site makes me realize how easy it would be for Timmo the Great to tank. All he'd have to do is bet on his chief rival (a young guy named Markku with a Charlie Chan fu), get down to the final two and then immediately bolt, so that Markku the Fu would win. He'd just have to make it look real. You'd hate to have the official go, "Uh, Timmo, do you mind waiting until we turn the sauna on first?"

By the time we arrived, Heinola was in full steam. This is a national event, televised no less, and the bars were already bubbling with insaunity. In one sidewalk bar about six guys, smashed already, with white-and-green painted faces and Viking horns, carried satchels full of reindeer powderhorn (*To help your horn stay stiff!* the sign on the pouch says. *Don't leave in mouth too long.*) and had bows of birch tied to their belts. Finns take them into the sauna and slap themselves on the back to increase circulation.

"We cheer for Redneck and Ironback," one face-painter named Samu yelled lustily. "One will be champion!" Saunists have nicknames? Who knew? What would my sauna nickname be? Babyback?

Samu was amazingly plastered for 11 A.M. "You are going *in?*" he slobbered at me, flabbergasted. "Look, I am Finnish and even I won't go in there!" Then he began hanging all over TLC, asking her what she does. "I'm a teacher," she said. He was right up in her face, two inches from it, wilting her eyelashes with his Finlandia breath, and said, "I'm a drunk."

Nooooooo.

7

At the registration table, they asked me to remove my shirt and then scrawl "82" on each of my biceps in Magic Marker, my competitor's number. I found out I was in a heat with the Tiger Woods of saunists, three-time champ Timmo the Great, the favorite. And that's when—as if on cue—his giant sauna-company-sponsored mobile home, complete with a sauna *inside* it, pulled up. The man even *travels* in a sauna.

Honey, I'm going down to the 7-Eleven for some milk and a shvitz. You want anything?

Timmo the Great waded through some autograph seekers (no joke) and arrived at the registration table carrying a quart of water. His skin is a kind of permanent cherry, and shiny hard, like a newly painted model car. He has long blond hair (turns out it protects the ears) and he's stout, stocky, maybe slightly pudgy. He is thin-lipped (also a very good trait for a saunist—Angelina Jolie would be awful at this). Timmo's pulse gets up to 200 bpm when he competes and he actually *does* train aerobically for this, riding the bike a lot and running. Have absolutely no idea why. He is also very quiet. You don't want to be a person who needs a lot of movement. You have to be happy to be just sitting, especially while your very organs boil inside you.

In short, he's the world's most famous saunist. He probably has his own signature-model back-birch-bow swatter.

With the help of an interpreter, I interviewed him.

Me: How much time have you been spending in the sauna lately?
Timmo the Great: Off and on, all day and night, about twenty sessions a day.
Me: Oh, my God! At what temperature?
Timmo the Great: Lately, it's been at about 140°C [or 284°F].
Me: Oh, good Christ! Do you drink a lot of water coming into the competition or what?
Timmo the Great: Oh, yes, about ten liters a day [2.6 gallons] the last three days. (He smiles at my reaction.) You, too, I'm sure, yes?

Me: Do you count beer?
Timmo the Great: No.

I was so screwed.

Because I was one of the first Americans to ever have entered the WSC, I did some very small interviews myself. There were all kinds of TV crews here—Ukraine, Germany, Sweden, and Russia. Variously, I pretended that I thought the competitors were *running* the sauna, or that it was a hot-tub competition, or that I had been training for this by eating jalapeños. I had brought along my six-eight shock-white-haired basketball buddy from Wisconsin, Bill "Thor" Pearson, who chimed in helpfully every now and then as though he was my publicist. "Rick does not have access to a sauna," Thor confided to one reporter. "So he's just been doing really, really long stretches at room temperature."

They nodded earnestly.

There were all kinds of odd entrants. A Japanese teen idol singer was there, name of Kazumi Morohoshi, and he was followed everywhere by his manager, his agent, his coach, some fans, and a Japanese TV crew. His odds were a ridiculous 13-to-1. I would have bet my last saunamobile against him. He was skinny and pale and much too pretty to suffer like my man Timmo.

The only other American entered was software designer Rick Ellis, formerly of the Soviet Union, who was so into this that he'd built his own sauna at his home in upstate New York. "I even considered putting $2,000 down on myself, but I couldn't figure out how." He said he's been training at 110°C (230°F) and had made it sixteen minutes once. His wife looked at him ruefully and shook her head. He turned to her, exasperated, "What?"

Suddenly, it was time for the heats to begin, and over 500 sauna fans took their places in the open-air theater. On stage were two hexagonal glass-faced saunas and two giant viewing screens. The gladiators for the opening heat were trotted out, all soaking wet from their freezing pre-heat showers. Ominously, a little man opened the door to the sauna and the six marched ruefully in, like drumsticks into a fryer. The fans chanted wildly. Sauna cheers? The mind reels:

We love Boris!
Here in the stands!
He'll never sweat!
He has no glands!

How bored must you be to watch people sweat? Actually, you'd be amazed at how fun it is to watch a grown man come apart like a $9 Walgreens sweater. How often do you get to see a man go from normal to nuttier than Ross Perot in less than ten minutes? We watched a Bellarussian, for instance, dissolve for our amusement. He started out sane, just sitting there, minding his own business. Every thirty seconds, a pitiless stream of water came out from a ceiling shower in the center of the sauna and splashed on the molten-hot rocks, creating a 100-percent humidity in the room that would melt gold. About two minutes in, our man started rocking a little. At three his eyes started blinking oddly. At four he began twitching. At five his eyes got huge. At six he started swallowing each breath like a gulp of scorching soup. Then he started glancing wildly around the sauna, as if to say to the others, "Are you mad? Don't you see what's happening? They've locked us in a Crock-Pot!" He started madly wiping his eyes and mouth. He reached his hands out to his thighs to rub them, then realized he couldn't, then did so anyway, crazily, wildly, like he was covered in lice. The judges flagged him once, then twice, and yet he would not stop rubbing. Then suddenly he lurched for the door and he was out and sanity and cool air whooshed back into his brain and suddenly he was normal and smiling again.

Kind of like watching Tom Cruise be interviewed.

One guy got in, sat down, and immediately bolted before they closed the doors. He grabbed the handheld mike and yelled, "Somebody farted in there!" Turned out to be a German TV comic. Backstage, a Dutchman held two bags of ice to his ears, thinking it might help. It didn't. He lost. I heard one guy coming out tell another who was going in: "Every second after six minutes is sheer hell." One German said his temporary fillings were rattling in his mouth the whole time. Not the kind of thing our hero wanted to hear before his turn.

In each opening heat, only two of the six moved on, and our friend Rick Ellis from New York went 8:03 to advance. I was waiting to congratulate him when I noticed something awful. There were two big patches of skin missing on his upper lip, just under his nostrils.

"Dude, were you by any chance breathing through your nose in there?"

"Yeah, why?" he says.

"Your skin is all gone under your nose! It's burnt off!"

He felt his upper lip in horror. He ran to the mirror. It was worse. The tops of his ears were split open and bubbling. Under his arms and on his back were bright purple patches. His forehead was painted bright red and blistering in front of his eyes. I took him to the beer garden to try to cool him off, but nothing helped. He was sweating like Pam Anderson at Bible study. "Man, I'm burning up. Even my tongue is burnt." His wife begged him to quit, but he refused. Said he trained too hard. She shook her head.

"What?" he asked.

And that's when they called my heat backstage.

Gulp.

On the way back there, I saw the great Finn saunist Leo Pusa, four-time champ, a stone-faced Greyhound bus of a man. I asked him for some quick words of wisdom before I went in, some secret he used to win all those titles. "I sat longer than the others," he said.

Let me write that down.

I vowed to do whatever Timmo the Great did. He took a drink. I took a drink. He stretched his neck. I stretched my neck. Three times, he took a freezing-cold shower backstage, so three times I took one, so that by the time I got introduced, I was shivering like a newly shaved Chihuahua. As they were reading us the rules, each competitor's fans were waving their nation's flag and chanting encouragement. Then I saw TLC in the crowd, mouthing, "Don't do it!" She'd said it before I left, too. "You know you can't win, so why not get out first? You're going to lose anyway!" She was right, of course. I mean, why try to out-eat Kirstie Alley?

I drew seat No. 6 near the door. Timmo the Great was No. 2. We went in and it was so instantly, shockingly, insanely hot, my brain just stopped working. It was like walking into a bonfire and pulling up a chair in the middle of it. It was like putting your face over the white coals of your barbecue and shutting the hood. It was so hot that if I owned this sauna and Hell, I'd live in Hell and rent this place out.

My strategy was to go in and keep time by the thirty-second water splashes, but that plan was scrapped approximately seven seconds in. It was just so goddamn hot I couldn't think. Thinking literally hurt. I tried to stare at the rocks and not blink, because blinking hurt. I tried to take very few breaths, because breathing hurt. Leo Pusa had shown me how to sit, slightly hunched, with your hands under their opposite arms, each of them protecting the fragile skin at the small of your back. But I was cursing Leo Pusa because it didn't help. Sitting hurt most of all.

My back seemed to have ignited. I was sure flames were coming out with each breath. I was convinced my ears were literally on fire, but if I moved even slightly, they would hurt more. I tried sitting up higher, but it was hotter the higher you went. I tried crouching down more, but then I was nearer the hideous, unforgiving rocks. It was so awful I could only wish Barry Bonds were in here. And then came the hideous, cruel, pitiless splashes of water, lasting maybe three seconds each. I did not count them. I looked at nobody. I heard nobody. I saw nobody, just the red rocks, glowing, laughing, mocking. I would sooner have my kidney removed at Jiffy Lube than this.

I decided to try to think of something to get my mind off the torturous pain, so I began to name every team in the National

Football League. But my brain needed a CTRL-ALT-DEL. I counted the New York Jets. Twice. I was just about to bolt into the fresh air when—miraculously—the tall skinny guy next to me in seat No. 1 suddenly jumped up and ran out! Amazing! I wasn't last! I had no idea how much time had elapsed—four minutes? Six? I was thrilled he had left, because I'd been told that as someone leaves, you get a lovely blast of cool air that gives you a five-to-ten-second respite. I looked forward to it with every cell in my body, but it didn't happen. Nothing. The two guards let the man out very quickly and nothing good came of it. It was dispiriting. Like opening a big Christmas present and finding homework. I made a promise to myself: When I get to the point where I can no longer stand it, I'll count sixty more seconds and then go.

Four seconds later, I decided I could no longer stand it.

So I started counting . . . One, two, three . . . I was pretty sure I was leaving out the "one thousand" between each number. It was the longest minute of my life. Now that I think about it, I'm not even sure I made it a half minute because I can't remember if I saw a water splash. I would've had to have seen at least one, right? I'm telling you, in that kind of furnace, your mind just goes completely Paris Hilton. At the count of sixty, I came barreling out of there too fast for the guards to let me out smoothly. I must wait for them! The bastards! May your daughter's wedding be in one of these things!

In watching other heats, I'd wondered why even the losers came out grinning and raising their hands in victory, but now I know. The cool air was so beautiful, so redeeming, so life-giving, that you couldn't help but smile a cantaloupe and pump your fist at just breathing it. You are out. You are taking in lovely, fresh, icy air. You could French-kiss Osama bin Laden.

I looked at the clock. Three minutes, ten seconds? 3:10? That was it?

"But you guys were in there a good six seconds before they started the clock," my buddy Thor said.

Well, OK, then. When did the first guy bolt?

13

"2:40."

Which meant I'd counted my sixty seconds in thirty. Which meant I would make a very billable lawyer.

I took a gloriously freezing shower and then watched the rest of the heat on the TV in the back. Timmo the Great and another blond Finn teammate of his (they wore a spa maker's name across the cocks of their Speedos) moved on to the quarterfinals, in just over 7:30. Seven minutes and thirty seconds? It horrified me. I'm horrified for *them.* I still cannot comprehend the pain of another four minutes and twenty seconds. Backstage, Timmo was surprisingly pink. I went up to him, chummy, and slapped him on the back with congratulations. He turned on me like he'd like to knife me.

Note to self: Slapping backs a definite no-no among saunists.

The Japanese teen idol had withdrawn. He made it to the quarter-finals, but now his trainer wouldn't let him go on. "It is good to care about sauna," the trainer scolded him, "but you must also care about the fans. You must care about the face they love." It was probably a good thing. The guy was so ravaged by prickly heat he looked like a Christmas candy cane.

Thor had come up with a great idea during intermission. He was going to cook lunch in the sauna. With two eggs in his hands, he entered, but the heat slapped him sideways and he lost track of what he was trying to do. He learned what I learned: ten seconds in that sauna and your IQ suddenly goes straight to NASCAR fan. He set one of the eggs on the bench and the other up on a shelf, but as he was doing that, he managed to sit on the first egg. It instantly began to fry. No, seriously, it *fried* like it was at Denny's. But it was too hot for him to try to clean it up, so he bolted out. "Oh . . . my . . . God," is all he would say.

Then there was the horrible tale of my friend Rick Ellis, the transplanted Russian from New York. He entered the quarterfinals with dozens of blisters on his body. We all told him he was crazy, but he had no trainer and his wife held no sway. He climbed into the dreaded hot box, while we watched, full of dread. As he was going in, he looked like some of the worst guys coming out. You could tell that, instantly, even he saw it was a mistake on the order of Three Mile Island.

"Man, I knew I was in trouble right away," he later said. "Soon as I sat down, I knew I had no chance. But when I felt behind my back and felt this big half-dollar-sized blister, I said, 'OK, that's enough. I gotta get out.'"

He was the first out, at 4:15, and when we greeted him, I nearly ralphed. He was melting like the wicked witch. His forehead, his lips, and his ears were giant sacs of pus. His tricep was riddled with pebble-sized blisters, dozens of them. So much skin was hanging off him he looked like the world's most successful gastric-bypass patient. His forehead was a science fiction movie. His nose was cooked like a forgotten kielbasa. And this was just what we could see.

"I don't know, man," I said. "Maybe you should go to first aid."

"Nah, I'm fine!" he insisted. "Although it does kinda hurt back here." He lifted up his shirt and there it was: this horrible, huge, pus-filled sac—the size of a $3 pancake—just hanging off his armpit. His wife gasped. TLC turned away in horror. Thor and I swallowed, fascinated. "Dude!" we both said.

When we dragged him to the first-aid EMT, the guy said, "You must go to the hospital. Within twenty-four hours, when these blisters break, you will lose lots of fluid. You will be highly susceptible to infection. We can't do anything for you here. It is too serious."

So TLC and I piled him into our rented Volvo and took him to the hospital, where, as we were leaving, his wife was shaking her head.

I got back to find I'd been inserted into something called the Wild Card Final, involving six qualifying-heat losers whose sufferings somehow amused the crowd enough to want encores. Wonderful. I vowed to go 3:11.

This time, somehow, it was even hotter, if that's possible. The bench was a wok. The skin on my back felt like the first night of Florida vacation when you've burned the bejesus out of your back and sides. But this time—counting all the cars I've ever owned—I managed to push through to four minutes, the second to come out again. My time was four minutes exactly. This time, the winner was a Bellarussian with about eight teeth total, who went just over six minutes. The guy who took second place, a milk-white Swedish guy I call Casper, was in the shower, looking defeated. "I knew I couldn't beat him," Casper said. "I think he was drunk. I'm not sure he knew what he was doing."

Good rule of thumb: never enter a sauna contest with someone who can't feel pain going *in*.

What's scarier than the men were the women. They were absolutely the meanest, toughest, and least attractive women this side of Rikers Island. They were all huge chunks of petrified wood, straw-haired and brute-faced, who looked like they just ate a lunch of boiled children and testicles. They were even more stern in the sauna than the men, and every bit as good. A former champ—Natalya Trifanova, also a Bellarussian—once actually lasted longer in the women's final than Timmo the Great did in the men's, but Timmo insists he could've stayed longer if forced to. There was talk that soon the women and men will compete in one field—like the Boston Marathon—to see, for once and all, who suffers best.

"Women are more tolerant of suffering by nature," Natalya grunted. "Because of childbirth and things like this." She is just slightly less expressive than a gulag wall. I asked her if she has a boyfriend. "Yes, we train together." No smile. No nothing. This is not a girl you buy lingerie for. Or propose to. She just comes over to your house one day and barks, "Today, we marry," slams you with a shovel, and drags you down to city hall by your haircut.

Our favorite woman, though, was a Finn named Leila Kulin who looked like Brun Hilda's lesbian aunt. She had these two long ponytails down each side and a huge ruddy face that could stop a front-loading Caterpillar. She was about five-two, 220 pounds, and most of that was face and the rest sheer will. She sat with her back to the piping hot bench, that face staring straight ahead, and she *never* moved. She didn't tic, she didn't flinch, she didn't lean, she didn't shift, she didn't even twitch. Her blood type was asbestos. Mannequins move more than she did.

So, naturally, the women's final came down to Brun Hilda and the brickish Natalya, and it has got to be the greatest final of all time, either sex, in WSC history.

At seven minutes, Natalya was starting to crack, fidgeting this way and that, wiping her face, checking impatiently on her feet and looking at the ceiling. Plus, she was competing against Mount Sitmore, Leila the Stone, who still hadn't moved, not a millimeter. Nothing. She's not human. She was born without nerve endings. Or a hypothalamus. Against this granite opponent, Natalya looked like a squirrel trapped in a microwave. She was blinking three times a second. She was gulping air. She kept shifting her haunches this way and that, trying to find a comfortable spot, but of course, the joke was, there are none.

Her eyes were wide as hubcaps. She moved to rub her legs as though they were on fire and she had to put them out, but she knew she mustn't, so she stopped herself. Instead she rubbed over them, over and over, an inch above them, as though rubbing *near* them would help. We were seeing a woman be electrocuted, battery by battery, right in front of our eyes. Finally, she couldn't stand it and she snapped. She started rubbing her legs up and down, madly. The judge jumped up and showed a red card and motioned her out. Disqualified. But get this—*she wouldn't come out!* The judge beckoned again. *Get out!* But she wouldn't!

She was a half-cooked rabbit trying to escape an oven. She tried to get up, but her legs were baked stiff. She was paralyzed! The crowd gasped. She motioned the officials to come get her, but they didn't! They seemed transfixed by the situation. Or perhaps the idea of walking into a burning building gave them pause. And what was the Stone doing while a woman goes stark raving bananas next to her? Nothing! The Stone was pitiless. The Stone didn't even look at poor Natalya.

You're dying? Never heard of you.

Natalya motioned the judges again, *Come get me!* At last, they went in—and you could see the heat hit them in the face like a Holyfield right—but they couldn't get her off the bench! It's as though she was glued! One try! Two tries! Nothing! She was going to die in there, in front of 500 people! Finally, they got a third man, and they were able to scrape her off the bench. They tried to get her into a wheelchair, but it was like trying to put an elm tree into a box, limbs were everywhere, and spasming. At last they folded her into it and raced her to the cold showers.

And now, finally, the Stone moved. And what moves! She leapt up off the bench in utter joy and barreled through the sauna door like Jesse James out of the Silver Dollar. She was bouncing up and down as they dragged off the poor quivering lump that used to be Natalya. Her winning time was 10:31, but you got the feeling she could've stayed in there and watched *Dr. Zhivago.* "I could've gone fifteen minutes at least," she said. I believe it.

Meanwhile, backstage, they were pouring icy water on Natalya from three different directions, trying to save her life. And standing there, quietly, in the fourth shower was the Great Timmo, who was going to compete in mere minutes in the men's final. He saw her and looked away, shook his blond head a little, took a cleansing breath, and tried to get the image out of his mind.

It couldn't be comforting. He was the next gladiator up after they'd wheeled the last one off in sixty-three pieces.

.   .   .

Just before the men's final, Rick Ellis returned from the hospital. He was a walking bandage. Gauze covered both ears, his entire forehead, his nose, every square inch of his back and sides, some of his chest, practically everything but his knuckles, which probably should have them. From the look on his wife's face, I knew what was coming next: They'll be turning his sauna into a shoe closet. "Guess I'm glad I didn't bet on me," he admitted.

Finally, the men's final arrived, and when the four pretenders bolted for their lives, it left the two favorites—Timmo the Great vs. Markku the Fu. They just sat and sweated and took furtive glances at each other, waiting to see if one of them would do the other the great favor of expiring so they could get the hell out. Ten minutes. Eleven. Twelve. It was a Hades standoff.

Suddenly, out of nowhere, Markku the Fu stuck his hand out sharply for Timmo to shake it. Timmo looked at the hand for just a moment, as if to say, "What the hell?" It was a shocking moment. The man was congratulating his rival on winning when the event wasn't even over yet! It was like Kobe Bryant stepping up to take the game-winning three and LeBron James offering his hand in congratulations just before he shoots it.

Timmo looked at the hand and shook it, whereupon Markku the Fu jumped up and flew out of the door, followed like a noon shadow by Timmo the Great, champion again, in a winning time of 12:26. Sounds like a recipe, doesn't it?

1. Soak in cold water.
2. Broil at 261 degrees for 12 minutes, 26 seconds.
3. Serve.

The winner was humble. "I was guessing he was better than me today," the great man said afterward, just slightly redder than a freshly cooked Maine lobster. "So I was surprised he shook my hand and left. Nobody's ever done that before."

And what did Timmo the Great get for suffering longer than every other person? Sauna speakers.

Hey, congratulations on eating more hams than everybody else! Here's your free ham!

I worked my way over to him, shook his hand, and said with a grin: "Well done!"

He stared blankly at me.

Note to self: Saunists don't like puns.

2

Ferret Legging

Generally, these are the five places you should *never* put a live ferret:

1. your garbage disposal
2. the pope's hat
3. the Upper Larchmont Junior League Annual Fashion Luncheon
4. your spaghetti sauce
5. your pants

And yet, against all sanity, I ignored this advice. In fact, in pursuit of the very real sport of "ferret legging," I allowed a woman to put not one, but two live ferrets down my pants.

While wearing no underwear.

Sober.

It's an experience I would . . . well, let me just say that through therapy . . . well, maybe I should just start at the beginning.

Ferrets (*groinica attachius*) are mostly tubular and often hairless and rather ugly, much like the lead singer for Midnight Oil. And those are their good qualities. They have teeth like barracuda and jaws like wood clamps and the attitude of divorce attorneys, which means if they chomp into you, there is a very good chance they are not going to let go until Arbor Day.

Ask Ben Stiller.

He was filming *Along Came Polly* with Jennifer Aniston, when a ferret he was holding (Aniston's character kept a ferret) chomped Stiller's chin and refused to release it. "I didn't do anything! I swear!" the poor man told reporters. "We were doing this final scene where I come running after Jennifer and I'm holding the ferret. He did this crazy turnaround thing and he literally attached himself to my chin and then he didn't let go. I had to get a rabies shot! I didn't provoke him at all. Their teeth are sharp, like razors. I mean, they're ratlike creatures. It was a horrible experience."

Incidents like this are what has earned ferrets the nicknames "piranhas with feet," "fur-coated evil," and "shark-of-the-land." They have a spine like a Roto-Rooter probe and more muscles in their jaws than a basement full of Dobermans. They have the same general DNA as Haitian loan sharks. They are not just vicious rats. They are vicious rats who know Roger Clemens' pharmacist.

Actually, ferrets are not really rats—though the resemblance is uncanny. They're kin to the polecat. They live for meat. Meat is to a ferret what heels are to Carmen Electra. In fact, the foot-long ferret (not counting tail) is so fond of meat that it makes an excellent hunter. A ferret can get down and through any tunnel a rabbit makes and chase it out the other end, where the hunter waits with hot lead. For a time in England, it became illegal to hunt with dogs, so hunters started using ferrets. Then it became illegal to hunt with ferrets, which, of course, didn't stop your average Nigel. The story goes that one day the game warden came walking up to a ferret-using hunter, who had nowhere to hide his ferret, so he dropped it down his pants. Must've been a memorable conversation.

Nigel (sweating): Hiyo, Warden Charles.
Warden: Hiyo, Nigel. Good day for hunting.
Nigel (biting own lip hard): Bloody good.
Warden: Are you aware there are quite a lot of odd movements
  in your crotch region?
Nigel (holding back tears): No! Truly?
Warden: Truly.
Nigel (shaking visibly): Well, I have a confession to make.
Warden: Oh?
Nigel: (weeping) You stir something in me, Charles.

Anyway, it turned out a warm ferret is a better hunter than a cold ferret and the pants-dropping practice caught on. This started an argument in the tavern one night among the lads. Who among them could stand having their ferret down their pants the longest? This probably begot a bar bet, which started a sport, which, 200 years later, somehow, involved me.

The rules of ferret legging are simple yet cruel: No wearing underwear. No declawing or defanging the ferret. Pants must be wool and clamped at the ankle. Belt cinched tight at the waist. No feeding the ferret beforehand. No drugging the ferret. No drugging oneself. Knocking the ferret off a particular part of your person is allowed, but only from outside your pants. Of course, this is like saying, "Lifting the steamroller off your foot is allowed," because there is almost no getting a ferret off a particular part of your person once it has its heart set on it. Some people use screwdrivers. I've heard of people doing it with scalding hot water. Also heard it doesn't work. The winner is determined in the same manner as an oyster-eating contest. The man who can keep them down the longest is the champion.

The all-time record for withstanding the pain of ferrets down the trousers is, believe it or not, five hours and twenty-six minutes by a furry little man in Yorkshire, England, named Reg Mellor. One time, *Outside* magazine asked Mellor if the ferrets ever bit his crank.

"Do they!" Mellor answered. "Why, I've had 'em hangin' from me tool for hours an' hours an' hours! Two at a time—one on each side! I been swelled up big as that!" And he pointed to a large can of instant coffee.

Not a comforting passage for the greenhorn ferret legger to read.

Ferret legging has fallen in glory since its heyday in the '70s. People decided it was cruel. Not to the ferrets, to the people. Great Britain banned it, which hurt a lot. Hell, you can't even own a ferret as a *pet* in California or Hawaii. Far as we could tell, only two places in North America still participated in legging: Winnipeg, Manitoba, and Richmond, Virginia.

But Manitoba apparently took too much heat from animal rights activists (if they only knew) and axed it in favor of "ferret racing," which involves ferrets running through a series of plastic pipes and tubes. Yuck. Now, if they released a rabbit two feet ahead of the ferret, perhaps coated in bacon grease, you'd have something.

That left Richmond, which was featuring ferret legging at its annual Richmond Highland Games & Celtic Festival, an event with the motto: "Music, Food and Large Men Throwing Stuff." The ad promised that these large men would heave giant rocks and flip telephone poles end over end. Plus, they'd be wearing kilts while doing it. Are those good things to combine? Kilt-wearing men and knife-toothed ferrets? Isn't that sort of like having R. Kelly at the Girl Scout Jamboree?

To get a little background on the coming event, TLC began e-mailing a woman from the Richmond Ferret Rescue League named Paige Collier, who informed her that I would "almost certainly" be fine, that yes, I would be putting them down my pants without underwear, but that everyone is only allowed to go three minutes and can quit anytime they want during those three.

That's it? Three minutes? Five hours and twenty-three minutes shy of the world record? I was almost, dare I say, disappointed. Then Paige Collier wrote, "Would you like to see bios of the competing ferrets?"

This came as a shock to the both of us. Ferrets have bios? Who knew?

"Send the bios," I said, since I make it a rule to know as much as possible about the things I'm putting down my pants. They came. Each bio arrived with a photo and a paragraph or two on the celebrity ferret. Here is an actual ferret bio she sent:

> Peppy . . . was surrendered to the Richmond Ferret Rescue
> League approximately 6 months ago, and is about 2 years
> old. He is a white, crimson-eyed male, who runs faster in
> reverse than drive. He is suspected to be deaf, but this
> doesn't slow him down. This is his first year participating
> in the ferret legging.

The mind nearly blows a gasket at all the questions this one single paragraph sends richocheting around the noggin. For instance, what does that mean, "surrendered"? Was Peppy involved in some kind of police/ferret standoff? And why is Peppy only *suspected* of being deaf? Couldn't you simply smash two cymbals next to his ears and see if Peppy jumps? Or is the fear of that reaction exactly why he's still only "suspected"? And, my God, if Peppy really is deaf, and he is *my* ferret, does that mean he can't hear me screaming? And why for the love of Christ does he go faster *backwards*? What kind of hideous hellbeast is this? And crimson eyes? Whose ferret was it, Charles Manson's?

There were more. *Mocha . . . is one of our therapy ferrets.* What kind of therapy does Mocha practice? Aroma? *Paco . . . is not particularly fond of other ferrets.* In other words, Paco has killed most of the other ferrets. *Tosh . . . has an awesome personality.* Oh, yeah, he does this great Jay Leno impression and, like, he's always got gum.

There was also very helpful and detailed information about such possible dungaree divers as Karma, Marley, Zack, and Clyde. If I had to pick one of those four to have down my pants, I suppose it would be Marley. Hopefully, he'd be higher than Snoop Dogg, find a small place to cuddle up near my ankle, and just veg. Thinking about it, I came up with a short list of ferrets I would definitely *not* want in my pants:

Fang
Adolf
Psycho
Lockjaw
Dahmer

Anyway, fast-forward to late October and me, at the end of a long ESPN road trip, pulling into the Richmond Highland Games & Celtic Festival to put a live animal down my pants in the pursuit of great journalism.

"Is that the deal Richard Gere was into?" my brother asked.

"No, no, different thing entirely," I said.

Then my son, Kel, weighed in.

"Ferret licking?"

"No, not ferret licking," I said. "Legging."

"Because I'd pay to see you do some ferret licking."

Smart aleck.

The festive color and pageantry of the Richmond Highland Games & Celtic Festival took place in a picturesque and charming . . . parking lot. No lie. A giant dirt parking lot next to the

Richmond Raceway Center. Inside was the answer to the question: Hey, whatever happened to all those geeks from high school drama club?

Turns out a highlands festival is kind of like a Renaissance fair, except way more plaid. Everywhere you looked were tanless people dressed in Elizabethan costume, most of whom weren't in any shows. Bulbous men in kilts. One woman was in leggings, a kilt, and a Darth Vader helmet. One entire pink, fat family of four was dressed identically, down to the little pom-poms on their socks—red kilts, white shirts, boots, and tam-o'-shanters. People walked around all day just *dying* to say something in faux Shakespeare.

> *Pimple-riddled teen in corn dog line, wearing palace guard get*
> *   up, complete with sword: Forsooth, their cupboard is*
> *   wanting ketchup!*
> *Pimple-riddled teen's mom: A pox on their tent!*

It was a great place to go on a diet, featuring Scotch eggs, Cornish pasties, Celtic ice cream (Hey, who wants a scoop of "whisky & clover"?), colcannon, and deep-fried Mars Bars. The many, many activities included punkin' chunkin', sheepdog shows, blessing of the animals, Kirkin' o' the Tartan, a woman playing the dulcimer, darp, and the psaltery, many swords, way too many bagpipes, and very large men in kilts heaving twenty-pound bales of hay with pitchforks over twenty-five-foot-high goalposts.

On the other hand, there was the giant Guinness truck with ten—count 'em, ten!—taps. And axe throwing! You could stand about twenty feet from a wooden bull's-eye and a wrinkled man with breakfast in his beard would teach you how to throw an axe, end over end, and make it stick. Five people would do it at once, only a few feet apart. Many of whom had just left the Guinness truck. And kids were welcome! Now, *that's* a sport.

I somehow made it past the Guinness taps over to *Young McDonald's Farm,* where the ferrets waited, about thirty of them, in a playpen, squirming and burrowing under, above, and through each other in a kind of massive king of the hill game. A gray-haired, very skinny woman wearing a fanny pack kept barking: "In the box, please! In the BOX!" It took me a minute before I realized she wasn't talking to the visitors but instead to Peppy, one of the ferrets, about his commode habits. The scolding went ignored.

On a table, there was a sign: *Did you know, ferrets catch human influenza and are used in scientific research? Without ferrets, we wouldn't have a flu vaccine!*

There should've also been a sign: *Did you know that without ferrets, 13.7 percent of the world's jokes wouldn't have a punch line?*

The very skinny woman wore a T-shirt featuring a doe-eyed ferret princess riding a rainbow against a field of stars—maybe from the My Little Ferret collection. It turned out to be Rita Jackson, one of the three women in the Richmond Ferret Rescue League. And so I tried, "Where's Peppy's leash?"

This, naturally, made me as welcome as a non-furry carnivore could be and got me instant introductions to the other League leader, Marlene Blackburn, an attractive brunette of about thirty-five. Turns out they have about a hundred ferrets in all in the rescue center, which is not a center at all but just three women who are willing to live with thirty to forty ferrets in their homes and, one would think, very few men. Rita alone had thirty-eight ferrets, two "free-roaming" ferrets, seven dogs, and three cats. Maybe not something you mention on Match.com.

I soon learned more about ferrets than any human should. For instance, ferret owners must trim their toenails (the ferrets', not their own) and—if you have any sense at all—sand down their teeth, which are a half inch long. Also, the center will take any ferret, even the hardship cases. They get all the survivors from the University of Virginia research projects, for instance. One time they got twenty-four. I'm assuming all of them had the flu.

"We're a no-kill shelter," said Marlene proudly. And it made me think, do the non-no-kill shelters advertise that? "Yes, we're a kill shelter. Just bring Nibbles on down and we'll box him up."

In all seriousness, it's wonderful that caring, patient women like these are willing to give these little furry creatures a home, because ferrets are just really, really unattractive. Two or three had absolutely no hair at all. They looked like Hebrew Nationals with feet. "Oh, those have adrenal cancer," Rita said. "They'll all get adrenal cancer eventually. Ninety-nine percent end up like Buster here."

Cool! How do I get one?

This was their seventh year doing the ferret legging at the festival. "At first we got so many complaints," Marlene said. "It made it into the paper and people started calling us and writing us and writing the district attorney's office saying it was cruel to the ferrets. The DA called me and I had to explain to him, 'Look, there's absolutely no cruelty in this at all. We only put them down for three minutes . . . They're therapy ferrets. They're used to it. Ninety percent of the time, they're trying to go up your pants leg anyway." Hell, that makes them no different than, say, David Spade.

"So they don't scratch and fight and bite when they're down there?" I asked.

"No! Most won't," she said.

Most?

"What do they eat?"

"Well, they're carnivores, so we give them meat-based ferret food."

"What, exactly, will they do while in my pants?"

"Well, no matter where you put them, they want to dig. They're scratchers and diggers."

Wonderful.

Just then a sweaty guy just slightly rounder than Bob's Big Boy spoke up. "I've had them accidentally down my pants, and right away, you want them out."

Accidentally? The mind reeled.

"Our goal is to get through the day without anybody getting stepped on, bit, lost, or stolen," Marlene said.

She'd be wrong. She'd be very wrong.

. . .

I had one large, fortifying Guinness and one nutritious pasty and walked over to the 100-by-100-foot ferret legging square, where the fans were already six deep, gnawing on their meat pies, anxious to see ferrets dine on those dumb enough to volunteer. A group of thespians called the Sterling Sword Players were the hosts of the thing, since the ferret women are not exactly, you know, *show people*. Now, usually I'd stab two forks in my eyes before I'd watch a group called the Sterling Sword Players, but these people were actually funny. And the main host, a big, bearded mall marketer named Kevin Robertson, was even funnier. He was hollering, "Ferret legging in five minutes! Be afraid! Be very afraid!"

I asked him how he got started being a professional ferret legging MC.

"Three years ago," he said between barks. "The director [of the festival] came up to us and said, 'We're going to have ferret legging here and we'd like you to be the host.' And we all thought it was a band. We're thinking, 'Ferret Legging? Cool name! Wonder what they play?' So the next day, up come these ladies with their cages full of ferrets. And we go, 'Excuse me, who in the world are you?' And they say, 'Oh, we're the ferret legging.' And we were just dumbfounded."

One time, a man who was mostly tattoos showed up and Kevin chose him. On went the sweatpants. Down went the ferret. Start the clock. Very soon, the ferret was rising back up above the man's waistband, poking his head up and looking around like he was trying to decide what he'd wear that day. So Kevin took the mike over to Mr. Tattoo and said, "He's done that three or four times now. Can you tell us how he's managing to do that?"

"Oh, he must've climbed up my Jacob's Ladder," Tattoo says.

Kevin replied, "What's a Jacob's Ladder?" Only as soon as he asked it, he wished he hadn't. Because the guy answered, "Oh, a Jacob's Ladder is the row of bars in my penis. I have them about every half-inch or so. He must've climbed up it."

OK, ewwww.

I asked Kevin who usually volunteers for legging. "Drunk people," he said. "One year, a couple women put the ferrets down their tops," he said. What's that called? Cleavage climbing?

When the square was packed to bursting, the three ferret wranglers entered like prizefighters, bearing six ferrets in handheld cages, plus an armful of sweatpants and blankets. Kevin started seeking volunteers. Amazingly, at least half the hands went up. He picked one guy, three women, and, as arranged, me. I was handed a pair of loose, gray sweatpants. Two guys held up a large blanket about neck-high around me to change behind, since everything has to come off—including underwear—and as I'm doing that, a thought occurs: five volunteers, six ferrets. What's the backup ferret for, in case there's accidentally some flesh left?

That's when Marlene came marching at me with *two* cages.

"Wanna take a risk?" she asked, grinning.

I nearly revisited my pasty.

"This is Spazz and this is Patrick," Marlene said, beaming. Spazz was all white and Patrick was a kind of sandy-white. They both looked nervous. That made three of us. "Spazz is an albino and Patrick is deaf."

"But aren't albinos really bad at seeing?" I asked.

"Yes," she said.

It's not comforting to know that soon deaf, blind carnivores will be in your pants, searching for meat-based ferret food.

I was made to face the crowd as it began counting down. My thoughts darkened . . . *What if the two ferrets get into some kind of argument and start fighting?* . . . nine, eight, seven! . . . *What if the blind one mistakes Coach Johnson for a scratching post?* . . . six, five, four! . . . *What if one ferret says to the other, "OK, let's eat one now and save the other for later?"* . . . three, two, one! . . .

I half expected Kevin to holler, "Ladies, drop your ferrets!" But Marlene just dropped them—wham—into my pants and tied up the waist of my sweatpants.

I'm trying to be honest in this book, even at great embarrassment to myself, and that is why I'm willing to tell you right now . . .

31

. . . I liked it.

It tickled! It was like dropping two Furbys down your pants. They both went for the right leg, foozled around some, then burrowed at my cuff until they escaped. Marlene kept picking them up and sticking them back in my pants. One time she dropped Patrick down, only he wouldn't go. He hung on to my waistband for dear life. Whatever was down there, he didn't want to go back. Then they'd both come scurrying out again. Finally, Marlene just came over and held my cuffs shut with each hand. A woman forcefully holding my pants shut? Sadly, not a first for me.

About halfway through the three minutes, one of them (it felt like Patrick) settled on a pattern of circling my left ankle, resting some, then circling again. Spazz (I'm guessing) climbed up my leg and settled in the crotch region and began, how shall we put it, nuzzling the walnuts. (Be a very good title for Ben Stiller's next movie, by the way: *Nuzzling the Walnuts*.) This was when the real drama began. Would he be satisfied with mere nuzzling? Or would he get curious as to taste and texture? My heart was in my throat. It was half thrilling, half terrifying, like getting a straight-razor shave from Naomi Campbell. Might turn out fine. Might turn out bloody.

But Spazz—lovely, sweet Spazz—remained tender to the end. I could see people charging for this. *Lap Dances! Peep Shows! Ferret Legging! $1 a minute!*

Honestly, it felt ashamedly good, especially with 300 people watching. It felt good enough that in Arkansas, we'd have to marry. Put it this way, it kicks hell out of Kirkin' o' the Tartan.

With Spazz happy and Patrick happy and me happy, I finally had time to see what else was going on, and that's when I noticed that one of the women—a blonde in a ponytail—was hollering, "No! Stop it! Hey! It's *biting* me! No, really!" The crowd was applauding and laughing and cheering.

"No, he's chewing my leg!" she kept insisting while people kept hooting with delight. Finally, Rita's nineteen-year-old daughter, Meagan, ran over to see her. OK, the truth is, the reason Meagan had to run over to the poor woman is that I asked her to take pictures of me. Ooops. By the time Meagan got her mother's attention and Rita ran over, the time was up. Rita yanked the woman's pants out of her hiking boots and the ferret bolted into the sunshine.

"Bad Spunkydoodle!" Rita scolded. The poor woman fell to the ground to see how much of her legs were left. "I don't know what happened," Rita apologized. "She's done this three times before without a problem!" The woman was trying not to cry. People were not laughing much anymore. Rita added: "He's had his rabies shots, so don't worry."

Sure! You'll walk with a limp from this day forward, but at least you don't have rabies!

Her name was Marta Rowe, thirty-four, and her leg looked like it had been used to stir a pot of porcupines. There were at least fifteen to twenty big scratches, a bunch of gouges, and lots of purple welts. It looked like a baseball bat that had been used to hit purple rocks. "He was chewing my leg!" she said, still a little befoozled. "I kept telling the woman, 'It's biting me!' but she didn't do anything! She didn't come over!"

Rita was still apologizing. "He's a rescue ferret, but he's very tame."

(Uh-oh. I know one little carnivore who isn't moving up to "therapy ferret" anytime soon.)

Marta: "I kept trying to grab its mouth."

And yet another ferret legger suddenly sees the wisdom of carrying a screwdriver.

By now the only other guy in the competition—a little mousy 5-8 guy with glasses—came over and chimed in with: "Mine was just curled up in the bottom of my pants the whole time. Nothing to it." Same with the other two women. "I haven't had that much action in my pants in years," gushed one of them. No problems at all. Maybe a love scratch or two. Only Marta Rowe got the full shark-of-the-land treatment.

Marlene said, "I think the problem was your pants were too snug. He wanted out."

The human ferret buffet was there with her husband—a large

ex-linebacker type with a beer in his hand—and her two kids, who had an expression on their faces you only see at home seizures. Marlene took the four of them over to the first-aid station, which featured an ambulance with the back door open and three paramedics, all smoking in lawn chairs. Seriously. They even had smokers' wheezes. Not exactly who you want coming to your rescue.

> *You: I think my heart has stopped and my right eye is over there*
> *near the stop sign!*
> *Richmond paramedic: Can we (wheeze) get to it in five*
> *(cough-cough) minutes, boss? We're on a (hack) cigarette*
> *break here.*

I asked them to guess how Marta got the cuts and bruises.

The woman paramedic growled: "Sword fighting?"

No, I said.

The fat paramedic grunted: "Axe throwing?"

No, I said. Ferret legging.

The randomly toothed paramedic flipped his Marlboro onto the dirt and said, "Now, that's just dumb! Those are wild animals you're putting down there!"

My beloved Spazz? Wild? How dare he?

They put some antibacterial ointment on Marta's leg and sent her on her limping way. Marta told her husband she just wanted to sit somewhere, so he led her off toward some picnic tables over by the axe throwing.

I was going to warn them, but I decided to go back to Marlene and ask if I could borrow Spazz and try it again.

Hey, I said it'd been a long road trip.

3

Bull Poker

If you were playing poker and were dealt a royal flush, would you fold it? Hell, yes, you would—if you were playing bull poker.

That's because in bull poker, the winner isn't decided by what kind of cards you have in your hand but what kind of grapes you have in your sack. In bull poker, four guys sit at a card table in the middle of a rodeo ring. A rank, 2,000-pound bull is released. When he and his horns charge the table, the last guy to leave his chair wins the pot. Like to see you bluff that.

When I heard about it, I knew two things: (1) I *had* to see this, and (2) I do not have those kinds of grapes. I don't care how much is in the pot, when that bull comes rip-snorting toward our Texas Hold 'Em, I'm off like a prom dress.

But then again, I'm not in Angola State Prison (Angola, Louisiana), which is one of the few places you can see bull poker these days, and I'm not doing a life sentence, which 85 percent of the fellas there are doing. So we humped our butts across the country to go to jail.

Two hours northwest of Baton Rouge, Angola is surrounded by alligators and bears and twenty-five miles of woods and rednecks on all sides. Most of the inmates are on full-ride scholarship—lifers—which explains why approximately 500 necks nearly snapped in half when TLC walked by the exercise yard in a tight "Wonder Woman" T-shirt and spray-on jeans.

Now, TLC is noticeable on Park Avenue, to say nothing of Angola prison. She's a kind of cross between Faith Hill and a young Cheryl Tiegs. A long time ago, she was Miss Teenage California, it just doesn't seem like it. About five-nine and built along the lines of Jessica Rabbit, she has Tahiti-blue eyes, California blond hair, and a swing on her back porch that would make the pope bite a hole in his hat. Not many women visit Angola, never mind a TLC, so you can imagine how many bench presses suddenly went unspotted.

TLC was nonplussed. A thousand eyes watched her approach. A thousand eyes watched her reflexively toss her long blond hair back. A thousand eyes watched her sashay away. Five hundred lower jaws lost the will to close. It was a little creepy knowing that night when the lights went off, 500 guys were going to be recalling that same image.

Our female PR escort took us to the chapel room of the prison church, and there we were, face-to-face with four murderers. No guns are allowed inside Angola, including on the guards. It was just two women and a jittery sportswriter against four guys who could take us hostage in three seconds. Break off a table leg. Block the door. Yank a shiv out of a boot. Anything. What was I going to do, squirt them with my fountain pen?

But the more we talked to them, the more relaxed we got. These four were all going to be in the prison rodeo the next day. More than 11,000 people would be coming with the fervent hope of seeing them stomped, trampled, and gouged, which seemed just fine with these guys. "I ain't scared of no bull," said Marlon (Tank) Brown, a spectacularly built twenty-nine-year-old black man from Baldwin, La., who was doing life for murder. "I don't mind playin' rough. I been playin' rough all my life. Hell, I hunted alligators. Alligators are worser 'n them." The escort reminded Tank that two years ago he had his leg stomped upon and his jaw broken by a bull. "Whatever," he shrugged.

Each man professed even less concern for his physical well-being than the last. "When that bull comes, I ain't leavin' the table for nothin'," said Jerry (Q-Tip) Tucker, a curly-haired white forty-three-year-old from Lodi, California, also in for murder. "Besides, the food's better in the infirmary."

An Indian lifer named Rich (Injun) Sheppard, of Shreveport, La., said: "There ain't been a year I weren't hit doing the rodeo. I broke my wrist one time. I pulled my groin. I tore my shoulder and my bicep on a bull ride once. By the time the bull poker event comes around, I'm already hurt. But I ain't goin' to the hospital 'til it's over. No way. You got a whole year to get better."

Turns out bull poker isn't the only suicidal event the inmates would be in the next day. There were seven others, each sounding more brutal than the last, including:

Bust Out, in which eight (8!) bulls and riders come flying out of the chutes at once, so that the prisoners have to survive not only their own bulls, but the hooves and horns of seven others. I didn't like their chances.

Wild Cow Milking, which sounds funny but may be the most dangerous of all. Eight teams of three inmates try to grab hold of a wild cow and milk it. First one to present a wet hand wins. "Them cows are worse than the bulls," Injun stated. "They'll kick you sideways. And they'll come over and kick you just to get their friend free."

Pinball, in which eight prisoners stand inside eight plastic hula hoops lying on the ground. The idea is not to leave your hoop when the bull tries to separate you from your pancreas. The last guy standing in his ring wins.

Wild Horse Race, in which inmates try to grab hold of a wild horse and ride him across a finish line. (The trick to controlling the horse? Bite his ear.)

Guts 'n' Glory, in which fifty inmates are in the ring when the bull is released. Tied between the bull's horns is a poker chip worth $500. Good luck trying to snatch it.

In short, it's a very good day if you own the local splint concession.

Why in the *hell* would somebody do any of this? Well, pride, for one thing. All their inmate buddies would be back at the prison watching them on closed-circuit TV, grading their falls on a scale of one (pussy) to ten (cheers from death row). "You can't turn yellow in front of those guys," said Q-Tip. "You'll hear about it for a year."

And don't forget the prize money. The year before, Tank won $200 in bull poker. What can you do with $200 in prison? Go to the commissary, where you can purchase such fine items as:

Can of soup, large—52 cents
Soup, small—19 cents
Tin of tuna fish—23 cents
Tin of sardines—27 cents
Socks—75 cents
CD player—$38

Also, the winner gets a real silver buckle with gold inlay. Plus, you're feted at the big steak-and-potato rodeo banquet and even your kids can come.

And how does one find the courage to win the bull poker buckle?

"I think about my bed," Q-Tip says. "I just try to sit as still as I can and think about my bed."

"I just pray not to be scared," said Heywood (Ironhead) Jones, thirty-three, of Slidell, Miss., in for second-degree murder. "One year I saw two guys run and I don't want that to be me."

"There ain't no point runnin' anyhow," said Q-Tip. " 'Cause the bull might veer at the last second and take the other guys out. You coulda won!"

Injun stated that you want to sit with your back to the chute. "That way you don't know he's comin'."

Of course, that leaves you prey to mind games. "I might tell him wrong," Q-Tip said. "I might go, 'He's runnin' straight at you!' Maybe he'll flinch and that'll make the bull go at him, see?"

Personally I was shocked at such unethical behavior in an American prison.

Of course, Angola is unlike any prison on Earth—how many prisons do you know with their own nine-hole golf course?—mostly because of its Puckish warden, Burl Cain, a pudgy red-cheeked imp with long white curly hair. He has the look of a teamster elf. When we met him, he was wearing a baseball cap that read: *Angola: A Gated Community.*

Cain stirred folks up when he started giving inmates a proper burial, complete with horse-drawn hearse, band, and a solemn march to the prison graveyard. Critics howled that murderers didn't deserve it. Cain howled back louder. "The man has done his time," he said. "The sentence was for life, not death, too. I'm not gonna kick his body."

Cain does all kinds of odd things. He started a Returning Hearts Day in which any inmate can bring his kids onto the grounds and play with them for the whole day. He says there's good in all of his men. The trick is to find it.

"Like this fella that brought you them cookies," he said, pointing at the deliciously gooey chocolate-chip morsel I'd just put in my mouth. "I call him Hop Sing. He's in for murder . . ."

I swallowed.

"... but he's a helluva cook."

I looked at the small Vietnamese man through the kitchen door. He wore an orange jumpsuit and leg irons. He was chopping meat with a butcher knife. There were no guards and no guns between us and that knife.

I stopped swallowing.

"I asked Hop Sing once why he done it. He said, 'Mr. Warden, a man whipped me two times. The third time, I was waiting with a gun. And Mr. Warden, once that automatic starts firin', it don't wanna stop.'"

Cain's rodeo is controversial, too. For one, people say it's just the lions vs. the gladiators in stripes. They say he's using the blood of the inmates to fill his coffers. Cain points out that (a) the inmates volunteer to do it, (b) nobody's died yet, and (c) most of the money goes to the inmates themselves. "These are men who've pretty much failed all their lives," he said. "But when the rodeo is here, people are cheering them! That does a lot for a man."

I suppose so. I just wondered what it would be like to be sitting in the rodeo and hear, "Hey, Mom! The guy who killed Dad just won Wild Cow Milking!"

Then there's the massive inmates crafts fair that comes with the rodeo—furniture, leather, and art, often sold by the inmate himself. Cain lets the minimum-security prisoners mix with the crowds, so you get inmate and citizen elbow to rib cage, over tables full of jewelry and bowls of chili. The inmates wear their usual: jeans, Timberland boots, and white T-shirts. The citizens wear their usual: jeans, Timberland boots, and white T-shirts. It can be a little awkward. Ironhead, for instance, makes his famous gumbo at the fair. One time, an old friend showed up at his booth. "Hey, man, I been lookin' all over for you!" the friend said. "Where you been?" And Ironhead looked at him and said, "Uh, in here."

One of the biggest criticisms of Warden Cain is that he's too nice to the people he kills. That's when I made the mistake of asking him where it happens.

He took us into Angola's lethal-injection chamber. Death was so present in that room, on you like a fog, that it immediately brought Hop Sing's cookies about two-thirds up. It was a cinder-block room, maybe ten feet by fifteen feet, with the killing table laid out like a crucifix. There were six belts up and down the length of the table and more belts for the arms and hands. There was even a small pillow for the man's head. After all, what if he gets a stiff neck? There was a little square hole that led into another room, where the doctors dispense the sodium thiopental. This way they don't have to see the man they're killing. All of this is watched from a room with about twelve chairs through one-way glass.

"It takes about a minute and a half for the drugs to kill the man," Cain said. "They usually take two breaths and they're gone. And then it's another four minutes for the heart to stop. But sometimes they'll surprise you. One ol' boy took his two breaths and we thought he was dead. And then, all of a sudden, he rose up and said 'Wow!' "

The warden holds their hand through the whole process. ("Now, if it was an electric chair, I wouldn't do that," he said.) Once the juice is flowing, he tells the man he has about ninety seconds and would he like to say one last thing? One man said, "Yeah, tell my lawyer he's fired."

I asked Cain if he's for the death penalty.

He tilted his ball cap back on his head and thumbed his rosy chin awhile and said, "Well, if there's one thing I've learned is it's all about the jury and your lawyers. O.J. proved that money gets you off. You know the inmate who served you the cookies? He's done worse than what some of the men who died here have done, but it's all about the jury. The older I get, the less I know for sure."

I asked about the red phone on the wall.

"That's for the governor," he said. "There's a code word he's got to use. That way we don't get any tricks. One time it was 'Exodus.' "

They use a generator so protesters can't cut the power. At one point, we heard an odd noise and Cain said, "That's the governor on the generator." And it made me think that sound could make for a terribly awkward moment some grisly day. The doomed man would be about to get the lethal dose when he'd hear an odd noise.

Doomed Inmate: What was that?
Warden: Oh, that was just the governor.
Doomed Inmate: The governor! Am I pardoned?!?
Warden: Oh, sorry. No, no. I meant the governor on the generator. My bad. OK, boys, hit it.

I could see TLC starting to turn white, so I asked if maybe we could get some fresh air. On the way out, yet another murderer, about fifty-five, was holding a taped-up box.

"Warden, can I borrow your knife?" the man said to Cain.

"Sure!" Cain said, happily handing over his gleaming six-inch pocketknife.

Inside my brain, I remarked, "Good Jesus!"

But the convict simply took the knife, opened the box, and handed it back to the warden.

I *really* needed a drink.

The next day was the biggie—the prison rodeo/craft fair—and if this isn't the weirdest craft show a person can go to, it'll do until one comes along.

First of all, how many craft fairs do you go to where, at the entry gate, they check under your car with a mirror, check in your trunk, and shine a flashlight on your floorboards? Inside was even stranger. Women with handbags were discussing clasps with guys who may have shot women in cold blood. Parents were putting their toddlers on ponies, to be led around a horse ring by grizzled men who may have fondled toddlers.

Sure was nice stuff, though. TLC and I bought two gorgeous oak rockers and a table from a guy doing life for armed robberies. We paid, get this, $200. Just before I gave him the cash, though, I took TLC aside and said, "Yeah, but what if this guy never ships them?" And she looked at me for a second and said, "Where's he gonna go?"

Good point.

Inside the rodeo arena made my collar a little itchy, too. There was a whole stanchion of medium-security convicts who were kept separate from the rest of the crowd by a twelve-foot-high barbed-wire fence, like jackals at a zoo. The competing convicts were in a kind of holding pen, too, just above the bull chutes. They wore jeans and old-fashioned wide-striped black-and-white prison uniforms, à la *O Brother Where Art Thou?* There were plenty of guards, but still no guns. Every time a convict cowboy was introduced they added his hometown, which always drew whistles and hoots of joy. I couldn't quite understand that. "Lexington! Whoo-hoo! That's our rapist! Go get 'em, Lexington!!"

One thing I now know about a prison rodeo, there *will* be blood, and it flowed from the first minute. The first event was Bust Out and eight bulls came flying out of their chutes with eight wildly clueless convicts trying to hang on. Most didn't. Immediately, out of chute 2, a convict fell hard and then, to our horror, had his head stomped on by the bull who'd just come out of chute 3. Honestly, it couldn't have taken ten seconds. Then, in the madness of thirty-two hooves stamping and flying and kicking and bodies flying hither and yon, two convicts came out and tried to drag the poor guy off. They looked like soldiers trying to pull a buddy out of Vietcong fire. They finally got him into an ambulance, bound for a hospital in New Orleans. This was bad. The guy was too smashed up for the prison hospital. As the ambulance pulled out, I noticed the eyes on some of the convict cowboys get huge, followed by swallows, followed by quickly turning back to the action to steel themselves. I've seen that same look at professional bull-riding events. Fear strikes deep, whether there's a number on your back or not.

Pinball was nearly as mad as Bust Out. The bull came out and, much to his great delight, found eight convicts in front of him, standing inexplicably steadfast in hula hoops. He snorted. They didn't move. He pawed the dirt. They didn't move. He drooled. They forgot to breathe. He looked like a tornado happening upon a trailer park.

He began with the man closest to him, who wouldn't leave his hoop and therefore took a vicious blow into the gut and out of the contest. Then the bull aimed itself at a second man, who—the image of Man No. 1 fresh in his mind—picked the hoop up around his midsection and ran. Nice idea, but disqualified nonetheless. The third man, no idiot, ran for his life and got gored anyway. Man No. 4 was either one of the bravest men I've ever seen or dumber than a sockful of nails. He took a hit and *still* wouldn't leave his hoop. Perhaps he misunderstood the rules, but he just formed himself into a little ball and kept getting butted by the bull, who got in four big licks before the clowns dragged the poor bastard off. Seeing that, Men 5 through 7 ran like hell when the bull merely looked at them. That left Man No. 8, Otis Strother. The bull never bothered Mr. Strother. I'm not sure the bull knew Mr. Strother even existed. Strother did nothing more than convince his size 12s not to leave their immediate vicinity. The moment No. 7 ran, Strother sprinted off right behind him, arms raised, joyous and free. The exhausted bull seemed glad to be shooed back to the pen, like a fat man at the end of All You Can Eat Night.

The Wild Cow Milking was won by a team led by probably the best cowboy in the prison, a fiercely blue-eyed convict named Dan Cook, forty, who was so handsome it was shocking, and who stared at you so intently you had to take a half-step back. If ever a man looked like a killer, it was Dan Cook. His face was covered in dirt and his ribs wrapped in tape. He was in Year 19 of a 125-year sentence for murder and robbery and seemed happy with it. "I belong here," he said, staring a hole right through me. "I hurt innocent people. I belong in here, not out there. What I did was senseless."

OK, then! Everybody's happy! Gotta go!

I looked up to see Q-Tip trying to ride a renegade bronco in the Wild Horse Race. He couldn't and twisted his knee doing it—had to be helped off—yet he refused to be seen by the doctors. "Too much money left out there," he said.

There must've been fifteen or twenty guys like that, aching and bleeding, but not leaving. I couldn't help watching one of them—a crew-cut, big-eared, skinny-as-a-2-iron kid who was doubled over in pain. His buddy was leaning over him, trying to get him to go to the ambulance, but the kid kept shaking his head. He was a twenty-two-year-old lifer from Louisiana—James Turner—who got himself kicked in Wild Cow Milking, then got stomped in the chest and legs in the bull dogging. "Why not get in the ambulance?" I asked him. I had to put my ear next to his mouth to hear him gasp the answer. "Trying to send my mom some money. (Inhale.) She got no place to live. (Spit.) She's just going from home to home. People's houses. (Inhale.) She's goin' blind. (Gasp. Pause.) My dad died last year. (Wince.) I gotta."

He'd wind up with $230 for the day. And two cracked ribs.

The crowd's favorite event was Guts 'n' Glory, which is like nothing anybody's invented this side of the Aztecs. This is the deal where fifty convicts get in the ring and try to get the nerve up to snatch the $500 chip fastened between the bull's horns. The bull was part furious, part panicked to be hunted by them. A bull cornered is not a pretty thing. It flipped at least five convicts in the air and flat-out ran over the haircuts of ten more. They chased that bull from one end of the ring to the other. They'd have it cornered and the bull would finally have no choice but to just come ripsnorting through them like a bowling ball through pins.

But then came Edward (ET) Trotter, thirty-eight, the best chip snatcher in all of Louisiana. Trotter's technique is the soundest and absolutely stupidest of all. He *lets* the bull run over him. But instead of covering his face and body as he's being trampled, ET reaches up, grabs hold of the rope, and snatches the chip as the beast drags him along under him. And this is exactly what ET did. He got three feet in front of the bull, challenging it to charge, and when it did, started backpedaling as fast as he could until the bull overtook him. As he fell, he grabbed the rope between his horns and hung on. The bull was head-butting him along the ground, dirt was filling ET's mouth and eyes, and yet his left hand was holding the rope while the right was loosening the chip. And he got it! When the bull was finally rid of him, ET stood up, raised his red right hand, and showed the crowd the chip.

"Man, that was a strong bull—strong and young," ET said, bloody and dirty and proud. "I just knew I couldn't panic. When he hit me, I made sure I was in the right spot to grab, but it [the chip] was tied on really tight. I really had to pull on it!" I looked at his left hand and there was a three-inch flap of skin laid open by the rope. Just to repeat: The man *purposely* let a bull run over him so that—while being trampled—he could reach up and grab a chip off its forehead. Who does that? ET does that. He not only won the $500 but Warden Cain gave him another $100 for bravery.

And yet even ET won't do bull poker. "Now that's suicide."

Speaking of which, this is the way the draw went down for it:

Seat 1: Robert (Rocky) Stewart, twenty-nine, in for murder from Natchitoches, La. Bull poker didn't seem to scare him any. "My mom asked why I'd compete in somethin' so dangerous and I tole her, 'Mom, I'm gonna die in Angola. The only rushes I'm gonna get are the ones I go after.' "

Seat 2: Q-Tip, bum knee and all.

Seat 3: Leonard Favre, thirty-nine, Bay St. Louis, Miss. In his three career attempts at bull poker he'd been tossed around like lunch meat three times. "One time a bull slung me way up in the air," Favre said. "That was a rush! Mostly, though, it feels like gettin' hit by a dang car."

Seat 4: Mathew Nightingale, from north San Francisco, twenty-seven, a two-time bull poker winner. One year his sisters came to watch and left crying. Now nobody comes for him. Good thing. His back would be to the chute.

The four started putting in their mouthpieces and flak jackets,

46

which were allowed for this event only. They were led out to the little red card table and red chairs. Each man was handed oversize novelty cards, about eight inches high, mostly kings and aces. Didn't matter. Cards are to bull poker what plot is to porn. As they waited for the bull to come out of the chute, the announcer said, "Only the lady who does their laundry knows how scared they are."

They sat absolutely stiff. They didn't even blink. The crowd held its breath. The chute opened. The bull exploded out and bee-lined straight for Nightingale. Favre only had time to say, "Here he co—" when the bull blew up Nightingale like a roman candle. It hit Nightingale so hard that he went flying straight through the table and straight through Favre. EMTs untangled the two of them and pulled them out, leaving Rocky and Q-Tip sitting like stones in their chairs, sans table.

I asked Favre what happened. "I can't remember," he said with a thousand-mile look in his eyes. "What happened? Something hit me in the head. I . . . ? Do you . . . ? I can't remember."

Later, Nightingale would remember too well. "That was a new bull. Never seen it before. I looked at the guy across from me [Q-Tip] and I heard, 'Here—' and then I got hit. I never had a chance to even brace. I never been hit by a bull that hard. I went flying into the other guy, Leonard. Hit him really hard with my elbow. It musta knocked me eight to ten feet. I started to panic 'cause I couldn't breathe. That's a little scary."

OK, so maybe back to the chute *isn't* the best seat.

In the midst of all that, the other two men sat in their chairs. Didn't move. Men being launched right in front of their eyes and they hardly flinched.

Rocky mumbled: "It's just me and you, Tip." Q-Tip didn't say a word. Maybe he was thinking about his bed. The bull circled back around, stopped about fifty feet away, and just stared at the two men, holding their cards. Rocky's back was mostly to the bull and Q-Tip's front was mostly to it. The bull must've thought what we all thought, which was: "Those idiots are *still* sitting there?"

The bull dug up the dirt a few times, lowered his head, and came straight for Rocky, who wouldn't budge. "I began to prepare for the hit," Rocky said, " 'cause I figured I was right in his line." And it seemed like the bull was going to knock Rocky clear to Biloxi, but at the last second, it veered, missed Rocky by not more than three inches, and smashed right into Q-Tip—and through Q-Tip—pitching him chair over hat five or six feet.

It was just a second before Rocky finally sprung from his chair, the victor. Maybe he couldn't believe it as much as the crowd couldn't believe it. He'd been spared for no rhyme or reason. He won simply because he hadn't chickened out, as any right-thinking man would have. He *knew* he was going to be walloped by a 2,000-pound bull running full speed and yet he didn't run. It'd be like sitting on the Dan Ryan Expressway and waiting to be hit by a Toyota Tundra.

He sprinted to the prisoners' pen, waving to the crowd, acknowledging the raucous roars of approval, like a gladiator leaving behind a floor of dead lions.

"I never thought about running, not once," Rocky said triumphantly. "You gotta push it to the edge. No limits. You sacrifice and take the lick to win. It hurts a little while, but not for long."

All of which begged this question: Rocky Stewart was in Angola in the first place for shooting a twenty-one-year-old girl named Wendi Long in the back of the head, twice, after she slapped his face after what he called "rough sex." So getting smashed by a bull only "hurts a little while," but getting slapped by a 120-pound girl hurts enough to fire two bullets into her skull?

It was all befuddling to Wendi Long's dad, Luke. He was amazed to hear of Rocky's heroics, amazed to hear about the silver belt buckle, amazed to hear about the money he won.

"He raped and murdered Wendi, lied about it, and dumped her body on the side of the road," Luke Long said from his home in Coushatta, La. "We were months looking for her. When we found her, she was just a skeleton. There was no DNA evidence to prove the rape, so we couldn't go for a death penalty. He [the district attorney] said he'd do hard labor. I pictured him out there in chains, busting rocks. I didn't know that someone who raped and murdered an innocent person would get to ride in a rodeo. That don't sound like hard labor to me."

Guess who's not coming to the banquet?

4

The Three-Mile Golf Hole

f I told you that you could take a 19 on a single golf hole and
it would take you five hours to finish that golf hole and at the
end of it, you would be so happy you would French-kiss a fat man,
would you believe me?

If not, then you've never been to Socorro, New Mexico, a patch
of cactus and rattlers an hour south of Albuquerque. Socorro is
famous for two things: (1) the world's only three-mile-long golf
hole, and (2) blowing stuff up.

They do both on Mt. Socorro, and it has slightly more explo-
sions than Fallujah. It's the home of New Mexico Tech, which con-
ducts antiterrorist demolition research for the Department of
Defense. They build fake factories, stores, and schools and then

blow them to Bejesus and back, using every assortment of letter, car, and backpack bomb you can dream up. The ground in town is constantly trembling. Someday, the gas station is going to blow up in Socorro and nobody's going to notice for three days.

One day a year and one day only, they stop the bombing and do something a little more dangerous. They play a one-hole golf tournament from the 7,243-foot top of Mt. Socorro to the thirty-foot hole at the bottom. And I mean *straight* down the mountain. So straight down the mountain that every year somebody has to be carried off the face, unless they come off in a chopper, which has happened a few times. Those are the lucky ones. Others go sliding down the shale, land in cactus, cut themselves on jagged rock, tumble down rock faces, and collapse of heat exhaustion under the pitiless New Mexico sun. Still, it's more fun than the British Open.

It's called the the Elfego Baca Golf Shoot. It's one hole—over 5,300 yards long—it takes half a day to play it, and by the time you're done, the thing you will most want to shoot is yourself, for ever agreeing to do the stupid thing.

Naturally, I signed up.

Elfego Baca was a nineteen-year-old Socorro sheriff who single-handedly took on a mob of desperadoes back in 1884. He chased them down, got trapped, held himself up in an abandoned adobe house for two days, waited for the mob to fire off all their 4,000 rounds, then came out and arrested them. Four thousand wasted shots? That's what a golf tournament is, right?

Driving into town, I couldn't help but shudder at the steep face of Mt. Socorro. At a BBQ that night, the realization that I was about to do something very, very dumb started to sink in.

A man so weathered by the sun you could screw his hat on came up and asked me: "You bring tweezers?"

"Tweezers?" I said.

"Yeah, tweezers. For when you fall in the cactus. There was a cameraman here once, fell right in a big cactus, and the reporter had to pull like 200 needles out of his butt. Gotta have tweezers."

No, no tweezers, I said.

A woman in a cowboy hat said, "You got new jeans?"

"New jeans?" I said.

"Yeah, 'cause of the horseflies. Some of 'em are so big they'll bite through your jeans. Hurts."

No, no new jeans, I said.

"I did it once," said a guy named Rich, sucking on a Bud. "By the time I got to the bottom, I couldn't walk."

Oh.

"Always follow your spotters," said Mike Stanley, the legend of the Baca, who won it all eighteen times he played it.

"Follow your spotters?" I asked.

"Yeah, that way, the snakes'll bite them first."

There was a long argument about whether I'd need to worry about all that since I probably wouldn't make it down in the first place. They told the story of the German TV guy who had to be carried off the mountain—fireman's style—by Anita, the 120-pound safety expert. There were reports that he was weeping.

Mike warned me not to lose a ball (one-stroke penalty) and to "be real quiet after you hit it. Don't call them on your walkie-talkie right away. Let them listen for the ball."

Walkie-talkie?

I was also warned against (a) contracting the hanta virus (mice), (b) severe dehydration, (c) getting lost, (d) falling into old mine shafts, (e) mountain lions, and, most of all, (f) letting your spotters get drunk the night before. I looked over at two of the three spotters I'd been assigned—Matt Majors and Jason Metzger, two young NMT explosion engineers—and they were well on the way to winning the blottery.

"We got your back, big guy!" one hollered. The other whooped with half his mouth, the other half occupied by his Budweiser.

Uh-oh.

· · ·

At 5:15 the next morning, I was picked up at my hotel by my only sober spotter, demolition expert Tony Zimmerly.

"You got Styrofoam?" he asked.

No.

"Or a piece of carpet?"

No.

Turns out you need Styrofoam and carpet to tee your ball up so you can hit it, since you're allowed to re-tee it anywhere within fifty feet of where you find it—no closer to the hole, which you can't see anyway.

At the range, where we were allowed to hit a few balls, I saw my two other spotters. They were still drunk. Their eyes were mere suggestions of eyes. They smelled like closing time.

Matt? I asked. Jason?

Apparently the volume in my voice was too much for Matt. The man was still drunk.

"Uh, yeah," Matt said. "We stayed until four at the bar, then everybody came to my house. Actually, uh, they're still there." They would be my eyes on this hellahole, even though those eyes would be bright red.

A big-shouldered, happy-faced guy in camo's came over, carrying a bunch of carpet pieces and Styrofoam.

"Heard you might need these," he said. "Name's Dennis. I'm dumb enough to play in this thing, too."

I took them, gratefully, and made up my mind to stay near him. Not because he was friendly but because he looked big enough to give me a piggyback if my legs staged a work stoppage.

One by one, I met the entire field of eight:

1. Primo Pound, thinnish. Really, that was his name: *Primo Pound*. Tell me that's not a great porn name. He was about fifty, gray hair, wearing a pair of gloves. "You'll want them once you fall," he said.

He also played his spotters smart. He brought a birdwatcher and a hunter. Is that better than two drunk guys?

2. Scott Jameson, a goateed grocer. I'd seen better swings on epileptics.

3. Mic Hynekammp, thirtysomething, ran the brewery/restaurant in town. He was dressed like he was going on Golfward Bound. Looked like he could hike from here to Switzerland. Golf? Not so much.

4. Bill Hall, fifty-seven, but in good shape. Decent swing, did it on a dare.

5. Chris Ritter, fifty-five, Bill's buddy, real estate broker from Albuquerque. Both these guys looked like good sticks. Both brought their wives as spotters and nobody else. Guys like that hit it straight. Stiff competition for me in the Best Middle-Aged Guy Award.

6. Caleb Gonzales, about twenty-five, good swing, good spotters, including his brother. By far the favorite. Won it the last two years. A slice of cheesecake in Dan Ackroyd's fridge had a better chance than I did against this kid.

7. Dennis Walsh, maybe thirty, family man and loaner of Styrofoam. People were picking him for second.

8. Yours truly, feeling a little nauseous.

"Do you want your own EMT?" Tony asked. I looked at him. He was not kidding. Not a good sign.

Everybody had three clubs. I had four—a driver, a 5-iron, an 8-iron, and a wedge. "You won't need all those," Primo told me. He was holding a driver and an 8-iron and that was it. He said that one time, a teenage girl did it with only an 8-iron.

"How'd she do?" I asked.

"She had to be taken down the mountain on a rope."

Anita, our safety coordinator, got us together and basically said we all had the intelligence of single-celled organisms for trying it. She warned us against just about everything under the sun, especially playing a three-mile golf hole down a mountain full of explosives. I asked Anita to tell me about the time she, a 120-pound skinny safety tech, carried a full-grown man down the mountain.

"Which time?" she replied.

We all piled in eight Suburbans and started the drive up. We passed "the chicken gun," the legendary weapon that fired chickens into the cockpit of a Boeing 727 to see whether a flying bird could crack an airplane window. (Frozen, yes. Thawed, no.) We passed airplane fuselages, old boats, all flavors of abandoned cars, small buildings, a helicopter, and an ersatz hardware store, all in the middle of nowhere. It was like driving through Hiroshima the day before the A-bomb hit. Everything we saw was doomed.

They dumped us out and had us hike a half hour to the first tee. That's when I knew one of the two older guys, Chris Ritter, was in trouble. He barely got to the top. He was exhausted.

The view was thrilling. The idea that we were going to play down it? A little terrifying. There was a small wooden platform hanging off a ledge somebody had built.

"What's that?" I asked.

"That's the tee," Dennis answered.

That thing? It was hardly big enough to pee off. It couldn't have been four feet wide and three feet long. You couldn't knit off it, much less hit a full driver.

Dennis handed me two crappy balls and took me to the other side of the pinnacle, where a couple of guys were hitting practice shots that would land God knows where. I'd never seen a golf ball fly that far, and I've covered John Daly. "You'll never hit a golf ball farther in your life," Mike Stanley had said the night before. But he said if you didn't hit it high on your first shot, you were going to give away hundreds and hundreds of yards. You could be on that mountain all day. I completely topped the first practice one and thinned the next one. I saw a rope in my future.

"What's par?" I asked.

Under the old rules—where you had to hit it where it lied and you played to a normal, tiny golf hole—par was about 50. Now, with the fifty-foot re-tee rule and the thirty-foot-wide hole with a twenty-foot-high flagpole, it seemed to be about 16, which happened to be the same exact par on any hole played by the late Speaker of the House Tip O'Neill.

Soon they were handing me ten yellow balls marked with a big "2" and the year "07" and saying, "OK, let's start." It was 6:30 A.M. and it had to be eighty degrees already. Let the story begin: Into Thin Error.

Primo went first, naturally, because his name is Primo. When it was my turn, I was shaking. The platform seemed even tinier as I stuck my tee through my piece of carpet and into my piece of Styrofoam. I radioed my spotters.

"You guys ready?"

Only Tony answered. Perhaps Jason and Matt had found a way to suck cactus juice.

I set my borrowed driver up to it—you don't think I was going to wreck my *own* clubs?—and made possibly the most in-the-barrel swing of my life. My head and hips hardly moved forward an inch. As a result, it went straight as Amy Grant and really high. Why don't I do this all the time?

Can I just tell you how fun it is to hit a golf ball 800 yards? I felt like Tiger Woods after a trip to A-Rod's medicine cabinet.

As predicted, Caleb hit the best drive—off a tee stuck in a broom. Dennis' was long, too. The two Albuquerque guys seemed worn out already and hit lukewarm shots, though they didn't fall off the platform. The grocer just cold-topped one. It dribbled fifty yards, all downhill, until it hit a rock. It meant his spotters were going to have to climb all the way up to it—a good twenty-minute hike, at least. And it meant he'd surrendered 750 yards. Sucked to be him, I guessed.

And then it was time to go.

Chris Ritter turned to his spotter and said, "Where's the path?"

"No path, man," the guy said. "You just go straight down."

He had a look on his face like he'd just seen Keith Richards naked.

I couldn't blame him. The mountain was all rocks and razor-back ridges and the promise of a big hard sun coming soon.

Those first few steps were all loose shale, so people were already falling on their butts. The only way to get down it at all with any speed—and speed was important, since the temperature was supposed to hit 103 by noon—was to ski down it. You know when you're skiing and you get stuck on a really steep cliff face and all you can do is make hockey stops, left then right, until you can finally point your skis downhill again? That's all I did. Hockey stops straight down for 400 yards, with my Nikes substituting for Rossignols.

It was about then I met my official scorer, who somehow was getting down it without a problem. She was an engineer named Aubrey Farmer, the girlfriend of one of Dennis' spotters. She looked about twenty-five, athletic, brunette, in hiking boots. She liked mountains, golf, and blowing things up for a living. In other words, the perfect woman.

Suddenly, we heard a "fore!" and we looked backwards 200 yards, where the grocer was topping it again. After a few minutes, he found it again and yelled, "Heads up!" Only this time, we just kept walking. We were right in his line, so I knew we were safe. This time he shanked it right. His spotters' heads sagged. There was only one channel for all eight teams, so you could hear everybody else's problems. "Uh, that one wasn't good," the grocer said over the radio. The last we heard him, they were still looking for it, which meant he'd be hitting five and we still hadn't hit our second yet.

It'd been a good half hour since I hit my first shot, so by the time I got to the ball, only Tony remained. The liver demolition boys had set off on another half-hour hike farther down—negotiating ledges and steep drop-offs—to the place where they guessed I might hit it. And when I found it, I had a new problem. When you're on a mountain face, it's almost impossible to find a place flat enough where you can swing the club without hitting a rock or a cactus or falling forward to your death. At last I whacked it again and sliced it right. And about three minutes later, Matt radioed: "Dude, you won't BELIEVE where your ball is!"

When I got there, they were pointing at something under a bush that grew out of a rock. Then I saw it. My ball was encircled by a rattlesnake. Just the body. The head and the tail were under the rock. Maybe it decided my ball was an egg? From the girth of it, we all decided it was big, maybe five feet. I stood ten feet away, happy to let it hatch and raise my golf ball for the rest of its life. Good luck to them both. Matt, though, kept taking my 5-iron and poking at it. I ask you, in the name of all that is holy, why would he do that?

"Hey! Knock that off!" I whispered in a panic.

"We gotta get the ball," he whispered back. "One-shot penalty."

I looked at Aubrey to see if this was true, even in this case. She nodded.

Was that something you wanted on your tombstone? *Died saving a stroke.*

And now comes a sentence never heard on *Mutual of Omaha's Wild Kingdom*: *Matt finally nudged the golf ball away from the venomous reptile and threw it to me.* I switched to a different one. Nobody likes snake juice on their golf ball.

Off they hiked again. I waited twenty minutes. It was just such an odd way to spend a day—like the Von Trapp family playing golf as they escaped through Switzerland. Tony said the third shot was crucial because if you mauled it, you could get over a cliff and then it could run down the mountain like snowmelt.

Tony went about 200 yards down from me and told me to hit it right over his head. Hell, it was straight downhill. I could FALL that far. I hit a screamer—an absolute rocket-propelled grenade—that looked like it might part Tony's hair. It sailed right over him and was still howling as it crossed the cliff. My primo pound of the day.

On the radio, there was a "Crap."

Crap?

"We didn't have anybody down there," Tony said.

It took me a good forty minutes to get down this time—sometimes going belly-down cliffs and feeling my way for footholds—all while holding golf clubs. Aubrey, though, looked like she was maybe shopping at Nordstrom's. Who *was* this girl?

When we got there nobody could find it. We looked for fifteen minutes and finally gave up. A lost ball already. My next shot would be my fifth. Winning was out of the question. Surviving was the best a guy could hope for now. I sat on a rock ledge to take a rest while the spotters scampered down to get in position again. I was just sitting there—swear to God—when I looked behind me and there it was, sitting under a ledge. As though it had decided to just get some shade and chill. I pointed wordlessly to Aubrey and then to the ball. Seeing as how there is no five-minute rule, she allowed it.

Buoyed, I let the next one rip, very high, a little leaky, straight downhill. I radioed ahead: "You guys got it?"

"Got what?" Tony said.

"My ball."

"Yeah, we're ready."

"What?"

"Tell us when."

"When what?"

"Tell us when you're gonna hit."

"I already hit."

"You already hit?"

"Yeah."

"Uh-oh."

"Please tell me you're kidding."

"No. We didn't know you hit. We have no idea where it is."

"No?"

"Absolutely no clue."

"Crap."

The thing was as lost as Amelia Earhart. We finally gave up. That meant I was now going to be hitting six.

"You really gotta make sure we know you're hitting," Tony said. You think?

Now it was really getting hot. My boxers were crawling. My jeans felt about 165 degrees. The horseflies were holding a convention near my ears. And I was losing my swing. My spotters were moving from the last glow of inebriation to the first shafts of headaches. They looked like they might stage a mutiny, especially after my sixth shot—a Newt Gingrich: short and right.

But that's when I saw Dennis.

He'd changed clothes already—"I sweat so much," he admitted. And no wonder. The guy hit it farther than many SkyWest flights. About 50 percent farther than me.

"Wow," I said. "What do you lie?"

"That was six," he said.

Holy cow! It was a revelation.

Self: *We're in this thing!*

Buzzkill self: *What about Caleb, you cheesebrain?*

"Seen Caleb?" I tried, casually.

"Uh, I think he's having trouble," Dennis said. "Lotta lost balls."

Holy Christ! You're a real boy, Pinocchio! I started picturing myself giving the winner's speech. *"Well,"* I'd say, *"if there was one hole that was the key to my round, I'd say . . ."*

I knocked my last shot off the mountain. From there on, it was strictly straight drivers over endless vistas of flat cactus and scrub. Dennis and I seemed to be doing it together, but he was denuding the ball and I was merely hitting it. It was like the difference between a Corvette and a Corvair. Still, it looked like he was having trouble finding some of his moon launches. The sun mocked us. It was exhausting, like being on a Lubbock tar crew. Were there no goddamn cart girls on this freaking hole?

"What was that, eleven?" I asked Aubrey, sweat pouring into my retinas.

"Thirteen," she said, hair blowing back from her face in her own spring breeze.

Finally, mercifully, the twenty-foot flagstick came into view. Another couple of slugs and Dennis and I would be there. Then I thought of Mike Stanley's warning: "I've seen guys get all the way down there and then blow two or three shots trying to get it in the stupid hole."

Didn't seem possible to miss a hole the size of a swimming pool. I guessed I was about 150 yards out—a 9-iron usually. Since I didn't have a 9-iron, I figured I'd try to punch an 8-iron. If I made it, it'd be 18. I saw Dennis was closer to the hole than I was, but who knew what he was laying? Caleb had self-immolated, was the report. The grocer was coming down by blimp for all anybody knew.

"What if there's a tie?" I asked.

"Play-off hole," Aubrey said. "From the bottom to the top."

Funny girl.

So I hit the punch 8 off the dirt, only it didn't punch, it ballooned. It went maybe a hundred yards, which left me still fifty yards out. Bummer.

I noticed that Dennis didn't make it in, either, but he was left with a ten-foot chip to a thirty-foot hole, which Jose Feliciano could make.

I hit the wedge, but I hit it off the toe, right, and it missed a hole the size of a basement foundation by a good five yards and was heading for a storage building. Whatever meager hopes I had were about to be crushed. Except—Holy Elfego Baca!—it hit a rock! And the rock sent it dead left into the hole! I was done! Five hours and ten minutes and I'd finally finished Hole No. 1 at scenic Socorro Municipal Link. My score: 19. I pretended to collapse like Pheidippides at the end of the first marathon. I was filthy, odorous, and spent. Aubrey, however, looked like she had just showered and was ready for Easter services.

I dragged my carcass to the shade of the building, where twenty or so were gathered.

Self: *You never know—you could win this thing!*

Undermining, evil self: *No chance. Dennis is a god. Weren't you watching?*

I tried to be non-chalant, but I'm sure I was chalant as hell when I threw out to Dennis, "So how'd you do?"

Dennis: "Pretty good, sixteen."

My heart fell . . .

"Except I had three lost balls."

. . . only to swell with joy again . . .

"Oh, so you had nineteen, too?" I said, cavalierly.

"No, that includes the three lost balls."

. . . only to be crushed in the end.

A little guy with a clipboard came up, shook my hand, and said, "I think you're gonna get second. You were right with him, until the bottom of the mountain. And then his two shots were worth about three of yours."

Horrid true self: *Told you.*

Caleb was already there and he had the red ass, figuratively and literally. He fell early. Slipped thirty yards down a cliff and ripped his pants and got cactus in his butt. And no tweezers! He wound up with a 22. "People are gonna ask me how I lost," he said, looking scornfully at his brother and two friends, "but I'm just gonna tell 'em: 'I didn't lose. Them other three lost.' "

Socorro Mountain: divider of men.

One by one, the other intrepid souls tromped home, like a lost battalion reunited at Arles.

Scott the Grocer showed up looking like he'd lost a fight with a Cuisinart. His arm had a huge gouge in it. How'd that happen? I asked. His spotter cackled, "Going for the Bud Light afterward." Scott looked bitterly at him.

Primo came in and announced, "I'm firing my spotters. But I found an arrowhead!"

I Hoovered about three very delicious, wet, and cold beers in about three very short minutes and then realized something. I never peed. The whole day. Teed off at 8:20, finished at 1:30. Never peed.

The stories started getting worse. Sharon, the wife of one of the older guys, Bill Hall, had to be carried down the mountain, a person under each arm. "I didn't quit," she insisted. "My legs did. I'd be walking along fine and they'd just give out. Next thing I knew, I'd be sitting down."

Bill's buddy, Chris Ritter, had to be escorted off after his *first* shot. Luckily, he was about a thousand yards from the road. The thirty-minute hike just getting to the top defeated him. Six hours later, he still looked like a guy four quarts low on blood. "Man, I was beat up before we even started," he said. "My legs got all rubbery. My golf was fine. I hit the ball right to [his spotter's] feet, but I couldn't walk down to her."

Mic, the bar owner, saved his best shot for last, a beauty that split the middle of the road. Only at the end, by the hole, the road becomes paved. So this miracle of a shot caught the pavement and bounced way past the hole. In fact, it rolled down the white lines another 400 yards, where it came to rest at a curve. That's when a truck stopped and a little seven-year-old boy jumped out of the passenger side and picked the ball up. The kid hopped back in the truck and his dad drove off.

Mic and his scoring official saw it all happening, screamed, jumped in a car, and chased the truck down. They pulled the startled dad over and tried to explain to him that the ball they'd picked up was Mic's, and it was in the middle of a tournament and Mic HAD to have it back. But the kid said no. So Mic got out his bag of balls and said, "I'll give you three of these for just that one of yours."

No.

"I'll give you ten!"

No.

The dad finally made the kid, who was still wailing when they drove off. They measured how far it was coming back and figured out the shot went 1.5 miles in total. Gotta be one of the longest shots since Alan Shepard's 6-iron.

The final scoreboard:

Dennis: 16
Me: 19 (that score would've won it the year before, mind you)
Caleb: 22
Primo: 22
Scott the Grocer: 25 (nice comeback)
Mic: 30 (plus two for moving the ball)
Bill Hall: 32
Chris Ritter: Nearly dead
Matt and Jason: Having a beer
Aubrey: Bluebirds tying ribbons in her hair

According to my calculations, if I played a full 18 at Socorro, I'd have shot 342 and it would've taken five days, three hours, and twenty minutes.

Or, in other words, one round with Charles Barkley.

5

Rock Paper Scissors

As a parent, you try to be fair. So, at our house, when there was a massive dispute that we couldn't settle between my middle son, Jake, and his brother or sister, I'd always say, "OK—Rock Paper Scissors."

And the tears would stop and both kids would smile a little and then I'd count, "OK—one, two, three, shoot!"

And every single time Jake would win.

And as he'd run off happily with the last cookie or the found football card or, later, my car, I used to think, "Man, that's the luckiest kid I ever met."

Until one day, years later, I was in Las Vegas, when a poker announcer named Phil Gordon bet me $10 he could beat me in

Rock Paper Scissors—best out of ten—and he'd *give* me the first two. And then he proceeded to fricassee me seven out of eight.

"How can that be?" I swore. "It's just pure luck, right?"

Wrong. Turns out Phil Gordon was a pro. In fact, Gordon hosts a $10,000 Rock Paper Scissors tournament in Las Vegas every year. It was the equivalent of having Betty Crocker walk up to you and go, "Wanna bet me in a bake-off?"

Gordon said I had a "tell" every time I'd go to throw Paper. He said I'd form it at the top of my arc and he'd see it and simply put down Scissors. He said newbie males always play a lot of Rock, so he countered with a lot of Paper. It reminded me of a bit from *The Simpsons,* in which Bart and Lisa are going to play Rock Paper Scissors for the last cupcake.

> *Lisa, thinking: "Poor, simple Bart. Always throws Rock. Every time."*
> *Bart, thinking: "Rock! Good ol' Rock! Nothing beats Rock."*

Gordon also said rookies rarely throw the same hand three times in a row. So anytime I played, say, Scissors, twice in a row, he knew on the next throw he could safely choose Paper and have zero chance of losing and 50 percent chance of winning.

"It's not luck," Gordon said, snatching my ten-spot. "It's skill."

And it hit me, right then, that Jake knew all those rules, too. It wasn't luck, it was skill. And that I was the crappiest parent since Jose Menendez.

It really gnawed at me how bad I was at RPS, so when TLC informed me that there was a world championship in Toronto every year—put on by the World Rock Paper Scissors Society, no less—I entered it immediately ($50, Canadian) and vowed to win it.

OK, not win it. But beat the knuckles off some people.

OK, win at least one match.

Pretty soon I was inside a world I never knew existed. For

instance, I never dreamed I'd read a quote like this one from Dave McGill, who won a $50,000 RPS tournament in Vegas: "God gave me a gift. It'd be a shame not to pursue it."

Wow. Really, Dave? Your fingers are a gift from God?

I never knew I'd know the names for all kinds of three-throw RPS gambits, such as:

The Avalanche—three Rocks in a row.
The Bureaucrat—three Papers in a row.
Paper Dolls—Scissors, Paper, Scissors.
The Tax Cut—Paper, Paper, Scissors.
The Bible—seven straight Papers.
The Guillotine—seven straight Scissors.

I never knew I'd wind up learning all the different variations of the game around the world.

- In a lot of countries, it's called RoShamBo.
- In Indonesia, they play Man Elephant Ant. The Man stomps the Ant. The Elephant crushes the Man. The Ant gets inside the Elephant's brain and drives it mad.
- In Philadelphia, some people play a two-handed game called Microwave Tin Cat. Microwave bakes Cat. Cat shreds Tin. Tin blows up Microwave. Not a good game, though, because using two hands means you can't hold your beer.
- My kids invented Bird Worm Gun. Bird eats Worm. Gun shoots Bird. Worm crawls inside gun and, uh, gums it up so the mechanism can't fire. OK, so they were six.

And I never thought I'd know all the official, certified RPS rules, including:

- No touching your opponent's throw. For instance, no taking your Rock and crushing their Scissors. No cutting up their Paper with your Scissors. No covering their Rock with your Paper. Apparently, your opponent has the right to then form Fist, and punch you with it.

- No launch pads. This is when you slam your right-handed throw into your open left palm. Very bush league. That was going to be a personal hardship, since that's always the way I did it.

- No throws are allowed except the Big Three. This would mean no Bird, Well, Spock, Water, Bomb, Matchstick, Texas Longhorn, Lightning, God, or Fire, a Copenhagen specialty in which league players can throw Fire once a month, killing everything. You can't go down that slippery slope. Pretty soon you've got Napalm beating Fire, Nuke beating Napalm, Nova beating Nuke, that sort of thing.

I learned, too, that people take this very seriously. Women get manicures. Competitors dress up. A man named Antony Maanum of Overland Park, Kan., keeps his hands in oven mitts during tournaments. His hands are *just* that hot.

I learned that there are long, heated philosophical arguments at international RPS conventions over things like:

- Does Rock "smash" Scissors or merely "blunt" them?
- Can a pair of scissors really cut an entire piece of paper with one snip or should, in fact, it take two wins by Scissors to defeat Paper?
- Should prosthetic arms be allowed? (World RPS Society president Doug Walker says no. "It opens the possibility for infrared technology to send signals to the arm to instantly fire a throw a millisecond before it hits, giving it an unfair advantage," he once wrote. No, he really did.)

You laugh, but the stakes can be enormous. Once, there was a fabulously wealthy Japanese electronics firm that decided to auction off its set of fabulously valuable paintings by Picasso, Van

Gogh, etc., which would produce a fabulous commission for the auction house that got the fabulous deal. The CEO heard proposals by the two biggie houses—Sotheby's and Christie's—and found both of them to be worthy. To settle the stalemate, he decided they should RPS for it. The auction houses sweated out what to do. Sotheby's decided it was just a game of chance and went with Paper. Christie's consulted the eleven-year-old twin daughters of an employee, who suggested Scissors because "everybody expects you to choose Rock." Christie's won the contract and the millions.

"Chance?" Pah!

As the 2008 world championships grew close, I began forming my impenetrable strategies:

- Strategy #1: If my opponent is a woman who looks nervous, new, and/or drunk, I'll throw Rock on the first throw. I knew women like to throw Scissors. It's the female equivalent of Rock. Something to do with sewing.
- Strategy #2: To make my opponent think I'm nervous, new, and/or drunk, I'll do really stupid things like sputter, "Now wait, is it one, two, three, shoot? Or, one, two, three and you throw on three?" And they'll think, "What a Velveeta brain. He's throwing Rock." And my Scissors will shred their Paper in one—not two—snips.
- Strategy #3: I'll watch for "double runs"— in other words, somebody throwing the same throw twice. For instance, if my opponent plays two straight Papers, I know he won't throw a third Paper. Most people, even the wisened, never throw three straight, so I can safely throw Rock. Will I be able to think that fast? Depends on how much I drink.
- Strategy #4: I'll take the advice of Graham Walker, also president of the World RPS Society (Doug's brother), who suggests an inspired strategy: Play the throw that would've lost to your opponent's last throw! He says inexperienced or drunk or scared players will subconsciously play the

throw that beat their last one. "Therefore," Walker writes, "if your opponent played Paper last throw, they will very often play Scissors, so you go Rock." Genius!

- Strategy #5: I'll throw more Paper than a *New York Times* delivery boy. According to statistics kept by God knows who, Scissors gets thrown 29.6 percent of the time, which is 3.73 percent under what you'd expect, which is 33.3 percent, which means Paper is safer than other throws. Then again, the 2006 winner, Bob "The Rock" Cooper, won with Scissors, so maybe not.
- Strategy #6: I'll mind-numb. For instance, if you want your opponent to throw Scissors, you "seed" the throw. You say a few words that begin with that letter— scintillating, super, sick—and they will often throw Scissors! Hey, it's science! If I say to you, "OK, you ready? Ready to rock 'n' roll? Right on!" You're thinking Rock, am I right? Which I will humiliate with my powerful Paper and laugh deeply.

I was ready.

The night before the tournament, Toronto was whippy and freezing but the designated RPS bar was heating up with some of the more famous teams and faces of the sport. There was:

- David Bowie's Package
- Running with Scissors
- Fistful of Sneer

We met Scissors Sister, who came all the way from Australia. We met former world champion Master Roshambolah, who, as always, denied he was the world-famous Master Roshambolah and instead insisted he was the Midnight Rider. "Master Roshambolah doesn't enter these anymore," he said in an odd accent.

Then we met a man who may have explained why. His name was Pete Lovering, a plain kind of man with a plain kind of face who was a walking cautionary tale. Lovering won it all in 2002—the first-ever RPS world championship—and then shrank from the enormity of what he'd done. Trying to live up to it became such a stone around his neck that he cracked under its weight. "The pressure just became too much," Lovering said. "I'd practice more and just get worse." He'd come to the RPS world championships and get eliminated in the first round year after year. "My kids would beat me constantly!" Then he muttered bitterly to no one in particular: "Them and their childlike minds." Now he doesn't play at all. It was like seeing Koufax at twenty-five with no slider. He slunk off into the night with his cup of coffee—a human blunted scissors, a defeated exhibit of what a what-have-you-thrown-for-me-lately sport can do to a man.

We met the much-feared Norwegian team—a six-person outfit whose "federation" had publicly stated that its goal was a Norwegian world champion by 2010. OK, so it's not exactly JFK promising a moon landing within ten years, but it's something. Naturally, as a proud American, I couldn't help but take on their champion, a twenty-five-year-old smug blond kid in a blue blazer and tie, no less. I pretended to have no clue what I was doing, tricking him into believing I'd throw Rock. Then I threw Scissors and slashed his Paper. Stunned, he came back with a pathetic throw—Scissors, the throw that had beaten his last one—only to find my powerful Rock waiting for him. You should've seen his coach's face fall like a globally warmed ice floe, as if to say *Uh-oh. We came 5,000 miles for this?*

My personal record at that point: 1–0.

Then I beat a Yahoo! girl who was giving out bottle openers if you beat her, which I did, although I think she was just happy to get rid of her approximately 1,000 bottle openers. (Personal record: 2–0.) I was feeling very good about myself until I met a woman from Philly named Mister Iz (pronounced quickly: "mysterious") who cleaned me out in two throws (2–1).

"My strategy is: Whatever I'm thinking, I do the opposite," Mister Iz explained. So if she's thinking she should throw Scissors, she throws its opposite, Paper. Or is its opposite Rock? Mister Iz didn't know. We didn't know. But since she'd just come from winning the Philadelphia city championship, she didn't want to know and instead guzzled a large portion of her beer, trying to shake the notion out of her brain. Maybe RPS is like golf or sex or Congress. The less thinking, the better.

Met the Minnesota Hustlers, too. They were two African American businessmen who bilk innocents for a hobby. They're that good. Word was that Tax Cut—so called for his penchant for throwing Paper, Paper, Scissors—had locked himself in a room and practiced against a mirror for an entire year. The duo's m.o. is to go into a bar—any bar—and dream up some dumb little argument with somebody there. For instance, if they see the guy getting the last Heineken, they'll say, "Oh, damn. I wanted that last Heineken!" The guy will feel bad, but they'll say, "Tell you what, why don't we Rock Paper Scissors for it?" Then they'll purposely lose. And then they'll say, "Dang! I KNOW I can beat you! Let me try again." And they'll lose again. Then they'll say, "Let's bet five bucks." Now the guy is feeling good and goes for it and wins and the trap is set.

Hustlers like them play "street," which is first guy to win ten hands, one right after another. No stopping. No time to think. Speed throwing. "You lose the first couple just to see what kind of patterns they throw," David (Tax Cut) Brookins said. "People will throw patterns and don't even know it. Soon as you have his pattern figured out, you bring down the hammer."

I saw it happen right before my eyes. Tax Cut's partner, the Reverend, was playing another Philly guy, a biblically bearded guy named Rhymes with Sausage. Rhymes with Sausage got off to an early 3–0 lead, but then the Reverend came stomping back. At one point—as they were furiously throwing—the Reverend actually called four straight throws of Sausage's. Just absolutely nailed what he was going to throw. He'd holler them out as they were coming. He'd yell, "One, two, three, Paper!" and there, magically, would be

Paper on Sausage's right arm. Then, "One, two, three, Rock!" And there was Rock. Sausage was powerless. The guy was inside his cranium. Sausage looked like a guy who'd just been told an earwig is eating through his brain. Four in a row! The Rev won 10–7 and $10, Canadian. Telling you, the Reverend is unholy.

He asked if I wanted to try it. I started to reach for my wallet when I got a less-than-gentle poke in the ribs from TLC. I then declined. Smart girl.

She proved that again the next day during my pre-championship practice session (Note: Practice rounds do not count in one's personal record.) We'd never played each other before. She'd done no research and yet she beat me about thirty out of forty. It was quite depressing. Her strategy? "I don't think," she said. "My mind is clear. I just go totally random."

"But an MIT mathematician says that humans are incapable of random th—"

"*Totally* random," she insisted.

The next night, the doors at the Steam Whistle Brewery opened to reveal what appeared to be a Star Wars convention crossed with a Hooters tryout.

It makes no sense, but, somehow, RPS draws crazy-hot women. Most of the RPS guys were skinny and pale and geekier than Pocket Protector Club. But they all had the right attitude for the thing, which was, drink hard, play hard, be ironic.

One guy was wearing a T-shirt that read: "I Rocked Your Mom." One was wearing a jean jacket with the right sleeve cut off at the bicep. His throwing arm, I guessed. One girl's shirt said: "Paper Is the New Rock." Another woman had on a tiara made of scissors. There was even a guy dressed like Edward Scissorhands. I was waiting for Rocky to show up. Helluva matchup.

Off to the left an entire team was doing warm-up exercises. I kid you not. Their captain was leading them through Rock lunges. Who knew?

I signed in and was given a number to pin to my shirt, the bottom of which was a ready-to-tear-off strip that said: "Currently Undefeated." After the TLC thrashing, I did not have much hope that it would remain attached long.

Over 700 combatants would be competing, single elimination, $10,000 for first place, $1,500 for second, and $500 for third, with an additional $1,000 to the winner of the "street wars" competition. Each player was given ten "street bucks" with which to gamble against each other between matches. These were the "street wars." Eventually, by the end of the night, somebody would have all of them, and the grand. I was thinking I should just go hand my street bucks to the Reverend now and eliminate the middlemen.

Round One

I went to Table N to find the seven others whom I would engage in hand-to-hand combat. Round One is actually two stages of matches, which meant that only two of the eight would move on to Round Two. One of the guys had on a big plastic-hair Johnny Bravo headpiece and was already well into replacing most of his blood with vodka. He was on Team Shocker. "We're just a bunch of idiots," said their coach. "Except him. He's an idiot, too, but he's really good."

Suddenly, the thing started and—I know this is hard to believe—I got squadrons of butterflies. "You think you won't," Mister Iz had warned. "But when it's you standing across from your opponent and the ref is there and all the people are surrounding you, it's scary!"

That's exactly what I thought, except when I stood across from my opponent I noticed he was not standing. He was sitting in a wheelchair.

He had long hair, a green T-shirt, and was drinking a Steam Whistle. His name was Russell Kinkelaar, twenty-eight, from Lindsay, Canada. He'd been in the chair since he was four, when a drunk driver hit him and his uncle. The uncle and the drunk died and Russell has been paralyzed from the waist down ever since.

Nice. If I lost, I was out. If I won, I'd have beaten some poor uncle-less guy in a wheelchair.

Now I was perspiring at the hairline. In the distance I could hear people doing cheers at some other table. And instead of concentrating on my first throw, I kept thinking, "What in hell does a Rock Paper Scissors cheer sound like?"

Fingers, Knuckles
Cuticle, Nail!
Our Phalanges
Never Fail!

There was a drunk guy standing next to me, part of my pool. "You nervous?" I asked.

"Nah," he slurred. "I come for the dollar beers. I drove all night, eight hours from New York, just to come to this."

I stared at him. "Uh, the beers are five bucks."

He looked at me like I'd told him he was drinking turpentine. Then he looked at his beer. "Dick nipples!" he said.

The referee called Russell and me forward. Thirty people gathered around to watch, and exactly one of them was rooting for me— TLC. And she was caving a little. "Well, wouldn't it be *nice* if he won?" she whispered. The ref drew us together. I sort of hunched over to be more down to his level. I heard somebody *tsk-tsk*. I guess this makes me an ass.

Nonetheless, I stuck with my plan, playing the rube. I asked the ref a few dumb questions. One was, "Is it best out of ten?" The other seven looked at me judgmentally. Then I threw Scissors, which cut his Paper nicely. The crowd groaned like I'd just put a kitty in a blender. I don't remember what the hell I threw after that, but I beat him in the first game, two out of three. Then he beat me two out of three. The crowd roared their approval. All tied. He spun his chair out away from me to steel himself (sorry—

figure of speech) and then back toward me. For the rubber game, I started with Paper, figuring wheelchair or no wheelchair, guys never open with Scissors with so many people watching, and I was right. My Paper clobbered his Rock. Then I threw Rock, for no reason at all—and he threw scissors and I was through Round One-A.

Very, very light applause and a few scattered boos. Russell took it well. "I tried to change it up in the first round," he admitted, "but nothing worked. Then you just beat me bad in that last game."

He looked so sad, I realized even I felt bad about beating him. But not as much as to not remind you that my personal record was now 3–1.

Right after us, the drunk guy from New York lost his first game and got so pissed he ripped off his entire bib. Safety pins went flying, except for one of them, which bent and poked him in the chest. And that's when I said, "Uh, it's best two out of three. You haven't lost yet."

He looked at me and looked at his crumpled bib and said, "Dick nipples!" And then he lost the next game, too.

Now there were four of us. I was first up, except my opponent—a tall, dark-haired guy in a button-down shirt—was on his cell phone. It was me and the ref and the crowd waiting for the guy to finish up. "OK, OK!" the guy was saying into his phone. "OK! Extra large! What? I don't know! Whatever color they have!"

The ref said, "Sir, you must hang up now or you *will* forfeit."

Guy on the phone: "I don't know! A hundred percent cotton! I gotta go!"

The ref started the game instantly and the guy was completely flummoxed and I beat him 2–1 in the first game and 2–0 in the second. It was over in less than ninety seconds. I used mostly Paper and Scissors. He was defaulting big-time to Rock. I was through to Round Two.

(4–1.)

"Dammit!" he said, looking at his phone. Turns out he was a lawyer named Matt Miller, and he had a strategy all ready to go, but the phone call screwed up his mind and he was playing before he could remember what his plan was. Who was on the other end? "My stupid friend telling me to get him a T-shirt. Threw me all off!"

But Miller still went over and bought him a T-shirt, throwing the $20 down disgustedly. That's a friend.

The woman impossible not to notice in the hall wore a giant pink beehive hairdo. It looked like a swath of cotton candy on top of her head and tangled up in it was a pair of scissors and a few pieces of paper. No rocks, though. Perhaps rocks sink in finely spun confectionary. Her name was Cody Bennett and her boyfriend finished fourth the year before. "He's been training me for thirteen months out of a book," said Cody, who was already half schnoozled. "If I win, I'm going to buy him a pair of cowboy boots." And if her boyfriend wins, maybe he'd buy her a 100-gallon hat.

Round Two

RPS bravado is wonderful to watch. One time, a guy skinny as a parking meter was about to face off against a rather buff opponent when he called "time out" and made a big deal of taking off his sweater, then rolling up the sleeve on his right arm. I mean, it was done with panache. Painstakingly, as we all watched, he got every wrinkle out. Finally, he was ready to go again and then—wait for it—threw with his left! And won! Do you love it?

One scruffy-faced guy had his right arm in a sling. Around him, teammates kept patting him on the back and saying, "It's OK. We understand. An injury is an injury, and if you have to withdraw, then that's the way it goes." The guy looked depressed and mopey, until suddenly he spun around toward his opponent, pulled his arm out of the sling, and pronounced, "Screw it! I'm going to play!" It was like the New York Knicks' Willis Reed coming out for

Game 7 of the 1970 NBA Finals despite brutal injury, except, of course, this guy was faking. Still, it energized his team—until he lost two out of three.

On the floor, I made the mistake of playing some street wars games and immediately lost both of them, cutting my ten bucks down to four. (Personal record 4–3.) That was bad ju-ju. I made my way to my next table to find seven more people intent on taking my $10,000. This time, my opponent was a tatted-up, pierced-out, stringy-haired twenty-five-year-old cook named Jessica, who didn't want to give her last name. Perhaps she was on the lam. "I've been practicing with my boyfriend for three months," she said. "But tonight, I'm really nervous and my legs start shaking and I can't remember what I'm supposed to throw. But everything has been working, so . . ."

I was thinking of using mostly Rock against her because she seemed pretty high and high women tend to default to Scissors. Unless, of course, she was playing the rube with me just as I'd played it against the poor guy in the wheelchair. But that's when a frizzy-haired young guy with a "Ba-Rock O'Bombers" T-shirt sidled up to me and whispered, "Dude, our buddy lost to her, she throws nothing but Rock! She must've thrown rock eighty percent of the time! She's terrible, dude. Throw Paper!"

Inside information! I decided to use it. My first throw was Paper. Hers was Scissors. I was already down one throw. I glared at Frizzy Guy. He winked an it's-gonna-work! My second throw was again Paper. Hers was again Scissors. Down one game already. I grabbed my haircut. What an idiot! The second game I threw Rock on the first throw and we tied. Then I threw Scissors, figuring it was time for her to finally throw some Paper. Imagine my surprise to see her Rock again. Down one throw already. I thought: No way she throws three straight Rocks, right? Who does that? This crazy spacey girl who tans by 20-watt bulbs, that's who. I threw Paper and there was her Rock again. Win for the good guys. Frizzy Guy smiled a see-what-I-mean? at me. I decided maybe he knew what he was talking about. Here came the rubber throw. Two Scissors. Tie. Would she go back to Rock again? Yes, yes, she would, I thought. She's that high. I threw Paper. And what did she throw? Scissors.

Dick nipples!

Game over. Match over. Tournament over for Our Hero. The ref leaned over and unceremoniously zipped off my "Currently Undefeated" strip. It was like in the Civil War, when the colonel rips off your epaulets and sends you out of the fort horseless.

(Personal record: 4–4.)

I was Steamed, so I went over to cool it down with a cold Whistle and who was there but Graham Walker, the president of the World RPS Society, the grand poobah of the finger martial arts. I told him what happened. His eyes got huge. "You idiot! You got conned!" he said. "It's the oldest con in the world. You got played by the second."

"The second?" I said.

"Yeah, she probably didn't throw Rock at all the first round. The guy was in cahoots with her. He's the second. So he tells you to throw Paper when he knows all she throws is Scissors."

I felt like Bruce Willis at the end of *The Sixth Sense*. Everybody knew I was a dead man except me. I stomped off looking for Frizzy Guy. When I found him, I took him by the shirt button and snarled, "Did you con me?"

"No!" he said. "I swear on my mother's grave!"

I didn't believe him. There was something in his eyes.

"I mean," he said, "we DO run a two-man con on the floor."

"What's a two-man con?"

Turns out a two-man con is when Guy No. 1 is throwing against the mark, when the "second" strolls up, pretends he doesn't know Guy No. 1, and says, "Hey, wanna play a three-way?" In a three-way, all three players throw and nobody wins a point until somebody cleanly beats both the other two. So if Guy No. 1 throws Paper and the other two throw Rock, that's a point for Guy No. 1.

The con is that the two buddies have a pattern all worked out so that they know exactly what each is going to throw. They keep it close, lose a few, but when the money gets big, Guy No. 1 eventually wins all the money, which he splits later with the "second."

So, sure they con people, just, you know, not me.

Round Three

The coat-and-tie Norwegian champ was crying. Literally crying. He had to bury his head in his coach's blazer. Turns out champions of national federations—Norway, Sweden, Australia—get a free pass into the third round. And he got one and was *still* gone after one (1) match.

"Pretty emotional, huh?" I asked.

"Oh, yes," he sniffed. "We aimed for three players to finish in the top sixteen this year. And so you see we have placed no one now. I am so sad for myself and my teammates and my country."

I could only hope the Norwegian federation brought the grief counselor.

On the floor, the atmosphere was blazing. There were dozens and dozens of street games going on. Huge stacks of street bucks were being held in the air while men in ninja hoods fought guys in sombreros with actual chips in the brims and salsa in the centers. And behind them, I noticed Johnny Bravo taking on somebody while his teammates chanted "Not your fault!" over and over.

"What's it mean?" I asked one of them.

"It means, 'It's not your fault when you lose to Johnny Bravo,' " the guy said. "He's just that good."

Brutal.

We decided we better get started winning the $1,000 street war game. TLC wanted to get rid of her street bucks as too many guys were hitting on her under the guise of "Wanna throw down?" So she gave her ten to me, which gave me fourteen.

I immediately went out and lost a match to a college girl (4–5). Now I had ten. I bet seven against a woman who looked nervous.

I won (5–5). Now I had seventeen. Bet it all against a very drunk man and won again (6–5). Now had thirty-four. Bet it all against a very small girl in rectangle glasses and lost on rock (6–6). Dead broke.

More hopes dashed on the knuckles of my lame fingers.

The street wars winner would wind up being a complete novice named Sara Harris, twenty-two, who lost all ten of her street bucks, then *found* eight on the floor and began betting her entire wad every time. "I never play," she admitted. "I'm not even entered in this! I was just trying to go home. I've got a big tax test tomorrow [at Toronto University]. But I couldn't lose!" She unknowingly beat some of the great hustlers in the country, including the Reverend, who lost a stack higher than his arm to her. I kept thinking of Pete Lovering and his "childlike minds." And what was her brilliant strategy? "I had no strategy at all!" she giggled. "I didn't think about anything!"

I looked at TLC when she said that. TLC looked at me knowingly. Perhaps RPS is a zen koan.

Q: What is the best strategy of all?

A: Nothing.

Round of 16

Among the people you'd know in the Sweet 16 were: Johnny Bravo, Cody (the pink-bouffant hair lady), one of the guys wearing chips-and-dip on his head, and the one-sleeved jean jacket guy.

The crowd was in a frenzy. The MC hollered, "The pressure is intense! There's not a dry mouth up here! And if somebody would bring me a beer that would be great!" But nobody did.

All in all, women kicked booty. Perhaps it's a hunch thing. They represented only a fourth of the original 700 and yet had three of the final four, with only Johnny Bravo representing the "good-ol'-Rock" gender. He faced Cody, the pink-bouffant lady, and lost to her, despite all his friends hollering "Not your fault!" Well, it was somebody's.

The Final

The Throw for the Dough came down to pink-bouffant Cody vs. a tiny thirty-one-year-old woman in librarian glasses and a checked sweater named Monica Martinez, a jewelry store owner from Toronto. She didn't even know she was going to enter the championship until the morning before. "She's just really, really competitive," her husband, Daniel Angel, said as he wrung his hands. "She started reading about it on the Internet yesterday. To tell you the truth, I'm not surprised she's in the finals. In fact, I'd have been in for a lousy night if she hadn't done well. She's that competitive. She's like this in every game: Euchre, Taboo, Cranium, Scrabble."

Cody, meanwhile, was good and properly tanked. And so it began.

The two women opened with Paper and tied. The jeweler stuck with Paper again and Cody beat it with Scissors to take a one-throw lead. Figuring it worked once, why not twice, Cody stuck with it and the jeweler topped it with Rock. Tie game. Then Cody stuck with it *again* and lost again. Game one to the jeweler. Odd fact: The jeweler hadn't thrown a single Scissors and Cody hadn't thrown a single Rock. But Cody got predictable with the Scissors—throwing it three out of four—and the jeweler carved her up for it.

In game two, they opened with two Scissors. Tie. Cody won the next with a very nice Paper over the jeweler's Rock to take a one-throw lead. But she didn't stick with it, switching to her weakness, dreaded Scissors, which hadn't won her a single throw the entire match, and the jeweler clobbered it with Rock. Now Cody was one throw from elimination.

I was thinking: "This would be a very good time for somebody to throw Fire."

Maybe the jeweler was thinking: "This pink Marge Simpson bitch is *never* gonna throw Rock!" Because she hadn't thrown one yet, not in seven throws. So the jeweler threw Scissors—knowing it was safe—and Cody threw Paper. And suddenly a woman who had never even *heard* of the RPS world championship until yesterday was your new world champion.

"I know it sounds weird," the jeweler told me afterward, holding a huge novelty check and picking confetti out of her hair, "but I can read people's faces. I've always been able to do it. I can totally tell when my husband's lying. On that final throw, I just read her face and I knew she would throw Paper. I just knew it! I don't know how to explain it."

So you didn't realize that your opponent had thrown five out of six Scissors at one point and never once threw a Rock?

"No," she said. "She did?"

Turns out Cody didn't know it, either. "I didn't throw Rock? Never?"

Sigh.

And then TLC pointed to her hair, where there were scissors and paper, but, fatefully, no rocks.

"Next year," Cody said, "I'm coming as a rock."

I decided I was coming back, too, only this time with a mind emptier than Britney Spears'. And I'm going to enter TLC, who will probably win.

But there's one question I never got answered, despite all my months of reading, practice, and competition, and it's a question that plagues those of us who pursue this sport with the passion and obsession it deserves.

How does a piece of paper beat a rock?

6

Women's Pro Football

C all me Stunt Monkey.

That was the name the SoCal Scorpions—the women's pro-football team—gave me, Stunt Monkey. Once a year or so, some unsuspecting male moron like myself will march in and want to suit up and try to tackle one of them or run through them, and the girls go out of their way to try to permanently separate him from his family ties.

"Stunt Monkey!" they'll holler, which basically translates to: *Let's hit this guy so hard snot bubbles come out of his nose!*

And you're thinking: Wait a minute. How hard can a girl hit, anyway?

And I'm here to tell you: about as hard as a recently tuned 2004 Nissan Xterra.

Sadly, I now know this from firsthand experience. It was my first day on the team. We'd warmed up and stretched and then, before I knew it, they'd suddenly formed a circle and started yelling, "Oklahoma! Stunt Monkey! Oklahoma! Stunt Monkey!" with the same lust in their larynxes as you might hear cannibals yell, "Boiling water! Fat guy! Boiling water! Fat guy!"

Soon I was being dragged into something called the Oklahoma drill, where the point is to drill somebody so hard they wished they were somewhere else, perhaps Oklahoma. This involved, on this day, one forty-nine-year-old rather lanky male (me) lining up against two twenty-something linewomen (them), each about the size of a Starbucks drive-thru. One was named Lela Vaeao, a Polynesian-American of about six feet and 280 pounds, a cousin to ex–San Diego Charger legend Junior Seau. The other was a young African American damsel who went about five-eight, 260, and seemed to have muscles everywhere up to and including her ovaries. A quarterback handed me the ball and light-footed it out of the way, which left me to try to run past these two front-end loaders on my own. That's hard enough, but the "field" I had to run through was only three yards wide—lined on each side by huge pads—which meant the two of them could pretty much fling their heft at me like great sides of catapulted beef.

When they hit me there was a happy whoop of "De-cleat!" from the rest of the Scorpions, which basically translates to: *We just hit this guy so hard both his cleats went straight up in the air in front of him while the rest of him went straight backward!* But that was not enough for these two. No, instead, when they hit me they kept me suspended in air, carrying me over the pads, outside the "field" another five yards, then pile-drove their 540 pounds into me and the ground at the same time. Their teammates roared and hooted and whistled like sailors at a strip show.

Definitely not the kind of threesome I'd dreamed about.

Lela was on top of me and not getting up. "Oh, geez, I guess we didn't hear the whistle!" she tittered into the earhole of my helmet and therefore directly into my right eye.

"Ngggh," I replied, since only one-third of my lung capacity was available.

This is the moment when most Stunt Monkeys pack up their cameras and their sound guys and go home. Did I go home? No. Did I give up? No. Why? Because I need thirteen full chapters, that's why. But when I stayed, a lot of the players looked at me in a whole new light, with a look on their faces that seemed to say: *You mean we get to clobber Stunt Monkey for two full days?*

When I told my buddies that I was going to play for a women's pro-football team, their first question was not, "What are you inhaling?" Their first question was, "Women play pro football?"

Yes, ma'am. Women's pro football has caught fire in this country like wet sponges. And to call it "pro" isn't quite accurate, since the Scorpions don't get paid to play, they *pay* to play—$500 each. Yet the team loses money like AIG stock. The owner, Ann Begala, had spent $500,000 of her husband's money the year before and took in $180,000, and that's driving the team equipment van herself. Hell, just having the required ambulance next to the field every game costs her $650. The coaches, manager, and publicist all do it for bupkus. They play on a crummy little field without goalposts at the Marine Corps Air Station Miramar in San Diego, and it's free because their coach, Dan Tovar, is a computer engineer there. Seven Scorpions made All-Pro the year before and had to take the bus to the game.

"You know what?" concluded cornerback Julie Beltz. "I'd play this game for free if I had to . . . Oh, wait. I do."

Every SoCal Scorpion has a day job, which can cause headaches, too. Sometimes, one of them will get pulled aside and taken into Human Resources, where there will be a grave panel of three people, who will sit her down and shut the door and whisper earnestly, "Is there trouble at home?"

And the player will go: "No, why?"

"Are you being abused? Because there are places you can go to be safe."

"Uh, noooo. What's up?"

And one of the board members will go, "Well, we see the bruises on your body. We see new ones all the time. And we just want you to know: We're *here* for you."

My new team generally handed out more bruises than they took. They'd gone 7–3 the season before in the WPFL (one of three pro leagues in America that year), made the play-offs, and gotten eliminated from them by the hated Dallas Diamonds, who wound up champions. We Scorpions really hate Diamonds. We hate Diamonds the way the French hate deodorant.

My two-day stint as a Scorpion tight end was scheduled two weeks before their season was going to start. The team's tireless handler, Jody Taylor, told me to just show up at the field and she'd have gear for me. She did. It almost fit.

"Where do I change?" I said.

"You're looking at it," Jody said.

So it was that we Scorpions proceeded to put on our gear right in the parking lot, over compression shorts and sports bras. And right away, I noticed how different it was from all the football I'd been around my whole life and also how much the same. So I started making lists on a little pencil and paper I hid in my sock:

THINGS YOU HEAR WOMEN PRO-FOOTBALL PLAYERS SAY WHILE GETTING DRESSED THAT YOU NEVER HEAR MEN SAY:

1. Is my makeup smudged?

THINGS YOU HEAR WOMEN PRO-FOOTBALL PLAYERS SAY WHILE GETTING DRESSED THAT YOU ALSO HEAR MEN PRO-FOOTBALL PLAYERS SAY:

1. Don't forget to take off your earrings.
2. Hell, yeah, I'd do her.

THINGS I HEARD WOMEN PRO-FOOTBALL PLAYERS YELL THAT I NEVER HEARD MEN YELL:

1. "Hit her like she stole your Cabbage Patch doll!"

NICKNAMES I HEARD ON THE SCORPIONS THAT I'D NEVER HEARD
ON ANY TEAM BEFORE:

1. Queenie
2. Whore
3. Bitchass

And that's about when I lost the stupid pencil.

There really was a girl on the team called Whore, by the way. She just enjoys sleeping around and isn't ashamed of it. "Look, everybody has to have a talent," said Whore, who asked that I not use her name or (cough-cough) position. "Mine is being able to deep-throat an entire summer sausage."

So there's *that*.

Lela only dates crackers. "They're cute!" says Lela, who, were she in the NFL, would be Tony Siragusa: large, crazy, and only stops talking long enough to crush spleens. "Besides, I can't date Samoan guys. I might be related to them." She'd like to date more, but there are obstacles. "When I tell them what I do, they seem sort of shocked. 'Oh, my God, I'm dating a pro-football player!' It's not easy."

A lot of the players get around these difficulties by simply sleeping with each other. The quarterback, Melissa Gallegos, sleeps with her center, Chris Carrillo. Sadly, since their offense is shotgun, she never takes a direct snap from center. That's another sentence you don't hear in the NFL much. *The QB and the center are lovers.*

There's just slightly more hooking up on a women's pro-football team than at a Sandals Caribbean. The second-string QB, Aisha Pullum, sleeps with a fierce little cornerback with a crew cut, Deuce Reyes. They both spit and swear and sit open-legged. In other words, they would both kick your ass. Deuce climbs poles for the phone company—(don't say it. Yes, the joke is there, but *don't* say it.). Aisha drives a cherried-out dark-tinted Chrysler 300 with the license plate QB7 (her number). Wide-eyed guys will drive up alongside her on the freeway and yell, "Sweet ride! Who's your boyfriend play for?" And she always yells back, "A—I'm gay, and B—I'm the QB!" Tends to end highway chat pretty quickly.

"Sometimes, it can be awkward," says tackle Katrina (Monty) Walter, a big, happy midwestern blonde. "Two girls break up and then there's a kind of riff about who's supporting which side. Men's teams don't have to go through that." Says Lela: "Like with Melissa and Chris. Maybe they'll have had a fight or something and Melissa will say, 'She's not snapping it right.' And Chris will say, 'Well, maybe she wants to play both QB *and* center. Is that it?!' "

You might ask, "What's lesbianism got to do with football?" And I'd say, "A lot." Just in my short time on the team, it mattered. For instance, in the scrimmage, QB Gallegos, who used to date Aisha, had on a yellow jersey, which meant nobody was supposed to touch her. That was a good thing for your reporter, because my man, a Marine named Crystal Stokes, was blowing past me like a roadside Cracker Barrel. Knowing that the defense couldn't really hit her, Melissa kept running these keepers that would get first downs. Deuce screeched, "Not fair!" and started yelling at the coaches about it. And everybody knew Deuce hates Melissa because of the whole Aisha thing. So Deuce started hollering at her, "Come across that line again and you're mine!" just loud enough that the coaches couldn't quite hear it. Then Melissa threw an out and Deuce picked it off for a touchdown, taunting Melissa afterwards.

"A lot of times it's like a divorce," says assistant coach Mark Ring. "There's some tense moments. I don't think Bill Belichick has to deal with stuff like that."

Sometimes, Tovar, who coached high school boys' football in Virginia, will be trying to discipline a player and the girl she's dating will get in the middle of it and start giving it back to Tovar. You know: *Why are you yelling at her so loud? It's not like she meant to do it! And who cares anyway?* Vince Lombardi would have a difficult time with it.

It gets worse. Melissa's new girlfriend, center Chris, used to be married to the Scorpions' old coach, a guy. But somehow, according to the players, he ended up with the backup quarterback, which convinced Chris to switch sides altogether and start dating women, namely Melissa. How would you like to be the newspaper beat guy on that team?

Good Lord, we're both thinking it, so we might as well get all the questions you have over and done with now. Go ahead.

Q: OK, on the road, do they have to, you know, share beds and stuff?

A: Yes. They sleep four to a room, two in each bed. Monty, who's straight, slept with a gay girl all season, no problem. "Not me!" says Lela. "I'm already trying to make sure I get a straight girl every road game this year."

Q: Do they all shower together, naked and stuff?

A: Yes, but they say it's absolutely not sexy. In fact, sometimes it can be downright disgusting. "We're trying to get a rule: You gotta shower in your bra!" says Monty. Lela: "I know! I mean, I'm big, but damn, you got to put that stuff away!"

Q: Do women do the same kind of horrible things to each other at the bottom of the pile that men do?

A: And worse. "One time a girl pinched my nipple!" Lela says. "My pads are too small and they came off in the pile, and a girl just pinched it! Hard! I grabbed her and took her down. I'm like, 'Do it again, bitch!' " (It might surprise you to know that Lela is a nanny during the day to a fourteen-month-old.)

Q: Do their boobs get hurt? I mean, can you hurt a boob?

A: Yes, and yes. A rookie tight end told me that once she turned around a little late on a pass and it hit her square in the right breast. "I had a bruised boob for, like, a week."

Q: How much of the team were lesbian? A lot?

A: The players I canvassed guessed it was between half and just over half, and it bothered some of the straights that people think *all* women's pro-football players are gay. "Look, we're trying to sell this sport for men to come and see," says Julie Beltz, an attractive straight cornerback, "and the people we send out to sell it are these crew-cut-haired, two-hundred-pound lesbians. I don't think that helps sell the image. Like, every time I'm in a bar with my friends, they tell guys I play pro football and *every time* the guy goes, 'Are you gay?' "

It's not easy for the husbands, either. The husband of Andrea Hubbard-Grant, a lineman, attests. "When we first started going out, I'd tell people, 'Yeah, I'm dating a football player!' Then they'd look at you real weird. I had to sort of watch it."

The MVP of last season's Pro Bowl was the Scorpions tailback Desiree (Dez) Weimann, who doesn't have a boyfriend. "I get the question all the time, three years out of four: 'You're gay, then, right?' The only year I don't get it is in a Summer Olympics year. Then they understand . . . But, I mean, I gotta be a guy's dream! Go have a beer and talk football with a girl you dig!"

It might also be her day job: mortician's assistant. She picks up dead bodies all day and takes them back for embalming, etc. "Death doesn't scare me at all," she says. "But it does make me want to get out and enjoy life. Football is in my blood." Literally. Her mom is president of Pop Warner Football and her dad is a coach in it. She must want it bad. She broke her neck playing it three years ago. After she recovered, she stopped for a while, but then decided life wasn't worth living without it. "It makes my heart sing."

She's a slasher, like a Warrick Dunn, Intel-chip fast and tiny. If she's not the best in the league, she's in the photo. I reckon she'd be a decent high school back if they let her play. "I think I'd *maybe* be able to play for a lower-division high school team," she says. "At *best*."

I don't know. She looked harder to tackle than Trig 501 to me. There were maybe three or four Scorpions I think could've started somewhere for a decent-sized high school boys' team. A receiver named Isis was big and fast and high-kneed. She was catching balls and then literally looking for people to knock over. Luckily, I was on offense, so I got to enjoy it. "Damn," I said to the girl standing next to me. "Nobody can stop her." And the girl went, "Oh, yeah, everybody's scared to tackle her." Been covering pro football for over thirty years and don't think I'd ever heard that before. I'm sure guys have felt like that before, though, but they've never said it.

> *Ray Lewis: Damn, that LaDainian Tomlinson. Nobody can*
> *stop that guy.*
> *Brian Urlacher: Oh, yeah, everybody's scared to tackle him. It*
> *looks like it might hurt.*

There were a few exceptions—players who were clearly out of shape, too fat, too slow, scared—but mostly they were solid and fundamental football players. "They're *so* much smarter than men," says Tovar. "They pick things up much quicker than men. I give them a play sometimes and they have it on the first run-through."

The offense is called Hustle and Flow and, I have to admit, we're hustling and flowing our little women's pro asses off tonight. Not me personally, of course. I'm being bottled up at tight end by this tiny little cornerback named Priscilla Flores who can't be much taller than my umbrella. But she's eyeball quick and all hands and strong for a midget. In between plays, I asked her if maybe she wouldn't do me the favor of choosing another profession so I could get open once.

Turns out she was a medical assistant. Her parents hated the idea of her trying out for the women's pro team, which is partly why she did it. "My dad said I'd never make it. My mom just hated the whole thing." But she'd played j.v. ball in high school and liked it. "Some guy tried to kiss me after practice," she admits. "Kinda weird. A teammate wanting to kiss you."

Making the team is just about the proudest she's ever been in her life, she said.

"Good," I said. "Now you've had your moment, go do something else."

Very few of them had any team football experience. We once had a female nanny who played starting quarterback for her eight-man high school team. It made for awkward neighborhood conversations.

Neighbor lady: Where's your dad?
My son: In the back, throwing passes at the nanny.

How many thousands of girls out there would love to play football but are told not to? Melissa is stocky, smart, and has a signal bark that sounds just like John Elway, yet her mother wouldn't let her go out for any kind of youth football. "She said the boys were too big." Just the opposite for Lela. She knew she'd be too good. "All my brothers were the stars of their high school teams. I didn't want to take that from them."

One linebacker, Tarrah Phillpot, got into it as a way of getting closer to her dad, which was odd, since he'd been dead for sixteen years. He was Ed Phillpot, the fine linebacker for the New England Patriots in the '70s who died of cancer when she was sixteen. "By the time I was born, he was done playing," says Tarrah, who sells Dodges during the day. "I kind of lost touch with him. This kind of keeps me close with him. I get to live now by the principles he taught me. Like, 'There's always somebody badder than you, so you have to give it your all.' "

Tarrah, a three-car-pileup sort of blonde, may also be the only former stripper in professional football. She was part of one "shoe show" or another for five years, from San Diego to Miami.

Any similarities between football and stripping?

"Well, yeah," she said. "The same locker room bullshit goes on in both. A lot of giving each other shit. And a lot of drama. Like when the other girls hate a stripper because she's taking all the tips. So they throw fruit punch on her best costumes."

Fruit punch?

"Yeah, fruit punch stains and ruins all your clothes."

I guessed that the big *difference* between stripping and football is that in stripping, when you pull groins, you generally make *more* money.

One woman joined the team to prove a point, that she could do it on one leg better than a lot of women on two. Born without the lower part of her left leg, right tackle Lindsay Hood came to the tryout and impressed the coaches but worried the ever-fretting owner, Ann. She remembers it like this:

Ann: I notice that you're limping . . . Is that a problem?
Lindsay: No, I have a prosthesis. Is that a problem?
Ann: No, no!
Lindsay: Look, if my leg falls off during a game, I have an extra
   one in the car and I'll leave it unlocked so you can go get it.

Again, stuff you just don't hear in the NFL.

Having tried to run through them, tackle them, and escape them for two days, they really are pretty good, two legs or one. I guarantee, if you happened to be driving by the naval base one day and saw this team scrimmaging you'd go, *Hey, high school football!* "My favorite thing," says Dez, "is to pop in a DVD of us playing—not say anything to anybody about who it is—and then see guys' reactions when we take off our helmets and all that hair falls out. They're shocked!"

The biggest difference I noticed between men and women's pro football is that women just laugh a lot more playing it. They're not quite as afraid of the coaches, not all gung-ho about everything. They chat and gossip when it's not their turn to run a play. None of them are trying to get to the NFL. They're not even trying to get to the CFL. They're just playing for the pure fun of it because they love the game and somebody finally gave them a chance to knock boobs, as they say.

The biggest similarity? They both hate having their real weights printed in the program. Guys lie heavy, women lie light. "One time, I put down '210 pounds,' " Lela admitted. "Everybody giggled. They're like, 'OK, Little Miss 210.' Because they all know I'm at least 280. My friend said, 'Why don't you just list 280?' And I said, ' 'Cause there's cute guys who read the roster!' "

Halfway through that first practice, I asked Monty if she thought I'd be good enough to play for them, if I were indeed a woman.

"Are you kidding?" said Lela, who hadn't been asked in the first place. "You looked just like a girl at first. I've been laughing at you all night. I'm like, this dude has no ass!"

"Seriously!" added Monty. "Your ass is all bony."

I'll take that as a no.

The more I played with them, the more I was starting to believe them. We'd been scrimmaging—offense vs. defense—for over thirty minutes and I didn't have a single catch. My hammy was hurting and my chest was still in the state of Oklahoma, and my back was getting tight. The practice was about to end. I was desperate. And that's when I had an idea. An awful idea. The Grinch got a wonderful, awful idea. I realized that the tiny, lovable cornerback Priscilla had probably not played much backyard football. Me, I'd played it my whole youth, teen years, college life, and every Easter, July Fourth, Thanksgiving, and, if possible, Christmas in the Cheating Is the Whole Point Reilly Backyard Football Classics. I asked for a time-out and huddled with my O.

"I gotta have one catch," I said to Coach Ring. "Can I call a play?"

He let me.

I came out of the huddle hangdog, looking like I'd been shot down, and ran to a lone wideout position on the left. I took a big sigh at the line and put my hands on my hips like I was going to pout the rest of the practice. But at the snap, I suddenly took off on a very quick two-yard buttonhook. It surprised my tormentor to see such a thing, but not much. Melissa looked at me, cocked back her arm, and brought it forward, just as Priscilla timed her step to intercept it and take it for a touchdown.

Only Melissa didn't let go. It was a fake. On her arm pump, I spun clockwise, being careful to hook our little Miss Priscilla with my right arm, tossing her forward—à la Michael Jordan on Utah's Bryon Russell to win the 1998 NBA Finals. No flag.

Don't cry, Young Priscilla. Your mascara will run.

I went long. When the little medical assistant realized she'd been bamboozled, her pulse must've stopped. *Doctor, Code Red!* I was five yards past her before she could even turn around. I might as well have been at an anthrax cupcake sale, I was so alone. Melissa tossed up a beautiful little spinning egg that nestled happily in my greedy hands a half second before the dreaded Deuce could race over to help. I high-stepped my way into the end zone—in the manner of a marching band major—leapt high and flushed it backwards over my head.

I really shouldn't have done that.

When I landed, something in my back began screaming, "You cretin!" TLC called a chiropractor that night and told him it was an emergency. He said he'd see us in the morning. Only Macallan whisky got me to sleep. Turns out I'd thrown my pelvis out. He reset it (first-ever expense report item: Pelvis, misplaced, $65), and said I was not to run, jump, or run pump-fake-hook-and-go's for three days.

Man, was it worth it.

I got razzed more than somewhat for not being able to practice the second day. I took all the meetings and hung out in the huddles, but I didn't suit up.

"Figures," Lela said when I told her I'd jarred loose my pelvis. "No ass."

But Monty admitted that I had a place of honor in Scorpion history. "You're the only Stunt Monkey who's stayed the whole practice."

And, thanks in large part to the example I set as a blocking sled and a cheat, the Scorpions had their greatest season ever. They won their final seven games, made the play-offs, finally knocked out hated, despised Dallas (spit!), and then gave the Houston Energy watt-for, 14–7, to win the whole WPFL enchilada. Quiche. Whatever.

Dez rushed for over 1,300 yards—including 172 in the title game—and was named the league MVP, for which she got a trophy of a guy. "Guess they don't make a lot of trophies with ponytails coming out the back," she observed. Melissa Gallegos—by far the shortest passer in the league—became the first QB in league history to throw for over 1,000 yards (1,520). And the whole team made it places no women football player had ever been: the sports section of the *San Diego Tribune* and the ten o'clock sportscasts. They each got a ring and Tovar got an unheard-of $500 bonus.

And then the league folded.

There was talk of till-dipping and misappropriation and lawsuits, but none of bringing it back. The Scorpions are now and forever the defending champions of a dead league.

"We're all going through bad withdrawals," says Dez. "Four or five of us went up and worked out for [the] Orange County [Breakers, a team in another league], but we just couldn't do it. It was just so—mediocre."

So Dez went back to normal life. She got a boyfriend and got a promotion, all the way up to crematorium manager. Still, she now has a moment that precious few men ever know: She is a world champion. And that can make a girl feel very alive indeed.

7

Chess Boxing

here is a sport—chess boxing—that sounded just so deliciously dumb I almost didn't want to know what it really
was. I just liked saying it, "Chess boxing."

Questions poured forth:

1. Was it two guys sitting at a card table in the middle of a boxing
ring playing chess? And maybe one of them goes, "Check." And
the other guy looks at the board, scratches his chin, and then just
cold-cocks the guy with a roundhouse right, sending him
backwards—bishops and queens and mouthpiece flying—and
adding, "You sure?"

2. Could a guy cheat in chess boxing?

Cornerman: *Ref, check his glove! Check his glove! There's a rook in there!*

3. Why combine chess and boxing? Can you think of two things that have less in common? Hey, I know! Let's combine scuba and baking? Bowling and colonoscopies?

4. Has a fan of one *ever* attended a match of the other? Although, it's true, the two do have one thing in common: Participants in both disciplines rarely have sex before a match. Of course, chess players don't have it after, either.

5. Did they do the chess and the boxing at the same time?
Breathless announcer: *Frazier's trying to get to his knight, but Foreman keeps slamming him with the jab!*

6. Could the ref step in and call it if it's getting out of hand?
Ref: *That's it! Fight's over! He just tried to move his knight diagonally! We're finished here!*

7. Was it live people—dressed as chess pieces—being moved around by two players standing in giant towers, with control of the square in question being decided by one piece boxing holy hell out of the other?

The truth, though, was nearly as dumb. Chess boxing involves two combatants alternating six rounds of chess (four minutes) and five of boxing (three) until one of them is either checkmated on the board or knocked out in the ring, or time runs out on the chess clock. In that case, whoever is ahead on the cards of the judges is the winner.
Does that make any sense?
The sport was never meant to be a sport in the first place. It was a piece of performance art by a Dutchman named Iepe Rubingh. He called himself "Iepe the Joker" and his opponent was a friend,

"Luis the Lawyer." Sitting in a fully lit, roped boxing ring, they proceeded to actually box, then play chess, over and over, much to the mouth-agape bewilderment of the art gallery audience. It was Iepe's statement about pigeonholing. It was so stupidly compelling—like *Celebrity Apprentice*—that they did it again two months later in Amsterdam. In that bout, Iepe was behind in the chess going into the last round of boxing and just decided to start throwing a slew of punches. He connected enough to make Luis the Lawyer loopy, so much so that when they got back to the board, Luis couldn't make sense of the pieces nor where they should go. Iepe won, declaring himself the world middleweight chess boxing champ, possibly because there *was* no world middleweight chess boxing champ.

Next thing you knew, sane people were under the mistaken belief that this was actually a sport—similar to NASCAR. Iepe began promoting the idea all over Europe and Asia, and suddenly, there was a whole mess of kings in the boxing world not named Don. Actually, Don King could clean up with this. Consider: Both former world boxing champion Lennox Lewis and current champion Vitali Klitschko both play chess, and play it very well. Can't you see the posters?

BLOOD ON THE BOARD!
Or . . . BLACK, WHITE, AND RED ALL OVER!
Or . . ."CUT ME, MICK. MY QUEEN'S TRAPPED!"

Anyway, I set out to meet a real, live chess boxer and see a real, live chess boxing match. And that meant Europe or nothing. America wasn't ready. There was one small club in Los Angeles trying to start up but getting nowhere. We decided the best of the European chess boxing seemed to be in London, where a former Channel 1 BBC reporter named Tim Woolgar was attempting to promote—and win—the UK's first sanctioned chess boxing match.

So I boarded a plane for England, hoping more than usual that the plane wouldn't crash, if only for the ignominy of it.

Mourners at funeral: Why was he going to London again?
My kids: Uh, well . . . chess boxing.

There are things you figure you'll never see in your life as a
sportswriter and one of them is a regulation-size boxing ring next
to four waterproof chess boards, full of pieces, with fighters alternating rapidly between knocking each other's blocks in and
knocking each other's queens off. But this is what I came upon at
the Islington Boxing Club in north London, top floor, far corner.
There were no chairs. Three men were on one side and three on
the other, each sweating like B.B. King onto the boards, trying to
clear their eyes so they could make their moves and punch their
speed chess clocks. Each player had twelve total minutes of time to
make his moves in the allotted six rounds of chess. If the player ran
out of time, he lost the match. Suddenly, a buzzer would ring and
they'd all put back on the one glove they'd taken off, and climb
into the ring and start punching each other.

Q: What wears one glove, chases queens, and isn't Michael Jackson?
A: A chess boxer.

Alternate answer: Woolgar, a square-jawed babyface with bangs
and rectangular glasses. In the ring, his feet were anvils, but his
punches jackhammers. Which was funny, because when he talked
about his style, he saw himself as a kind of British Muhammad Ali.
"I like to dance, stay out of reach, and hammer with the jab, like
Ali," he said.

And I think I look a lot like Brad Pitt.

As a youth, he was decent—his record was 1–1. "But my second
fight, my opponent was really starting to get annoyed with all my
dancing Ali stuff. He got really mean. I knew I had to do something different pretty soon or I was dead. So I threw a straight
right. I didn't feel it even hit. It was that good. The guy went
straight down."

At nineteen, his trainer said he either had to turn pro or quit. So
he quit and went to college. "Too bad, though," he rued. "I have a

very strong jaw. I used to ride my bike to school and had no basket for my satchel, so I'd carry it in my mouth. I can take quite a punch because of that, you see."

Of course, it's hard to tell if he's lying. He promotes himself as thirty-five in chess boxing when he's actually forty-five. The bastard—he actually looks thirty.

Woolgar first heard about chess boxing while trying to be charming with a delectable woman at a party. He was mentioning to her that he loved chess and would she fancy a match sometime? "Oh?" she said. "You should try chess boxing. My boyfriend loves it!" And before he could tuck his ego between his legs and escape, the boyfriend was there going, "Oh, yeah, chess without boxing is crap!" Next thing you know, Woolgar was at a match in Berlin and hooked.

"I just found it to be pure excitement," he recalls. "Thrilling, really. Could the one chap who was the better boxer finish off the chap who was a better chess player before they had to go back to the board? I loved it!"

After the fight, he asked the promoter if he could join a club in the UK.

"There is no club in the UK," the German said.

"Bollocks," Tim lamented.

"So why not set one up?"

Soon he was quitting his BBC job to chase the kind of dream that when you tell people about it, they spit out their Guinness. Why quit a good job for something so patently ridiculous? Because he loves it. He loves it because, he says, the two disciplines are so much like each other. In both sports, fatigue can lead to dumb moves and a loss. Each uses combos. Both involve setting up traps for each other in hopes the opponent doesn't notice. Jab, jab, then the right. Jab, jab, then the right. Jab, jab, fake the right, left cross.

Except chess is far more brutal than boxing, Woolgar says. "Boxing is the sport of gentlemen. In chess, there's no quarter asked nor given. We have a champion, Frank Stolz. He lost his crown to a nineteen-year-old when he blundered his queen. I know Frank would've rather been knocked out cold than do what he did, to lose his queen. It was humiliating for him."

Chess genius Bobby Fischer used to find great pleasure in "the moment when I break a man's ego." It's a truism: Men prefer their nose broken to their pride.

Exhibit A: In Greensburg, PA, recently, two men were playing chess when a Mr. Zachary Lucov became so humiliated at his blunder that he announced he was going to kill himself. He grabbed a .40-caliber Glock and pointed it at his head to prove it. The other participant, a Mr. Dennis Kleyn, leaped to stop him. They struggled. The gun went off and a bullet went through Kleyn's arm, came out the other side, and nearly killed Lucov's nine-month-old son, who was playing on the kitchen floor. Why the baby was playing on the kitchen floor at just before midnight is unknown. In fact, the whole story is sketchier than TMZ. As Lucov was leaving court a few days later, he was asked by reporters if he tried to kill himself. "I don't recall wanting to," he said with aplomb.

Seems like that's something you might remember.

The best boxer of the six I was watching was a kid named Sascha (the Flascha) Wandkowsky, an unemployed German student who rides his bike to the gym every day, practices his chess and his English, and scares the bejeebers out of anybody who has to face him in the ring. In his last bout, he disfigured a British guy. "He concede," Sascha says in his spotty English. "He had a little broken bone in his face, I think. Just leettle. But he was bleeding all over the board, so he stop the fight."

Those annoying leettle broken face bones.

"My chess is good, but I always make mistakes," says Sascha, who is just a beginner in chess.

Me: Well, that figures, because you're probably tired from
   the boxing.
Sascha: No! I make them in the first round, before the boxing!

So his strategy is to stall on the board and attack on the canvas. He will take as long as he can over each chess move, figuring he will rearrange your cerebellum quite quickly in the ring. Generally, the ref will nudge you if you haven't moved in twenty seconds, DQ you in thirty or forty. If Sascha the Flascha can get a guy in the ring for at least two rounds without doing something really stupid to lose the chess first, he usually wins. "In my second bout, I am almost out of time. I am at 11:50 and he had only use only fifty seconds. I managed to have only ten seconds left when the four-minute bell go off. This poor guy he must put on his glove and come back to ring. And then I knock him out, I really knock him out."

Which brings up a hole in the entire sport to my mind.

Why couldn't a person who never plays chess—like Mike Tyson—simply stall for the first round of the chess and then knock his opponent out colder than a flounder in the first ring minute? I put this to the club's best chess player, a five-six brainiac named RajKO (get it?) Vujatovic, one of 200 actual chess masters in all of London.

"Well, he could," RajKO declared. "He would just have to get through the first four minutes of chess without doing something so completely stupid that I was able to mate him before we got into the ring. And that'd be very, very stupid. I think I'd need at least into the third round of chess to defeat a simple beginner, unless he just had no idea how to stall."

And in the ring?

"I'd just have to run," RajKO said.

I wanted to test this theory, but Woolgar's insurance wouldn't allow me to box. So I played RajKO in chess just to see how long I could last. I know as much chess as I do Swahili, which is to say almost nothing. I only know how the pieces move. He beat me in about six minutes—thirty-one moves—thus proving himself wrong. He could've defeated me in only two chess rounds and he'd need only to survive one round in the ring with me. Although I was an idiot about it. I was taking five seconds between moves, not thirty, so it all went much too quick. But considering that in his sparring sessions, he sometimes threw both fists at once, I think that's all I would've needed.

I asked RajKO what the other chess masters think of him chess boxing. "They think it's bonkers. Bizarre. Chess players are not supposed to be punched in the head." Actually, it might make an interesting pay-per-view telecast.

Fischer has now absorbed twenty-two straight punches in the head and yet he still has Joe Frazier in check!

After the boxing, the six combatants went back to the board and proceeded to sweat all over it. The pawns were nearly drowning. It was a rubber board, but still. I asked Woolgar how often he cleans the boards, which looked like something that should be sent immediately to the Centers for Disease Control. His answer? "Uh, never."

A lot more matches end by rook than hook, and there's a reason for it. It's much easier to topple a king onto the board than a man onto the canvas. It takes some real skill and strength. These guys don't have it. It's mostly a lot of, "Ow! That hurt!" and keeping the distance of a Cessna between each other.

It's hard to explain how awful most chess players box, but this may give you an idea:

The two best chess players—RajKO and a very skinny Chinese guy named Doug—began sparring. They both employed the seldom-seen double-punch strategy. RajKO was closing his eyes when Doug threw a punch, which never got past RajKO's gloves. He had them both in front of his face and yet Doug wouldn't go for the body. Nor would he extend his arm fully when punching, nor turn his fist into the punch. His salvos had all the power of a man on his deathbed reaching out for one last brownie.

Hanging over the ropes, trying to give them pointers, was the London senior lightweight boxing champ. He'd come up from below just to help out a little. He hollered at RajKO, "Try the jab!" And—get this—they both *stopped* and looked at him. Just stopped boxing, turned to the guy, and said, "What?" It's the equivalent of a coach yelling at his running back to "Hit the hole!" and the running back suddenly stopping—ball in hand—running over to the sideline, and saying, "Say again?"

The real boxer just buried his head in his hands.

At one point, Doug got a punch through RajKO's double-fisted closed-eyes wall and bopped him on the nose. The receiver looked surprised and his eyes watered a little. He dropped his hands and rubbed his nose. Doug looked like he'd just shot a bunny. He apologized and then actually reached out and rubbed Raj's nose, too. I thought the boxer from London was going to cry.

Afterward, there was this exchange:

Me: Who would be the greatest chess boxer in history?

RajKO: Pound for pound? You'd have to say [world chess champ Gary] Kasparov.

Me: What?

RajKO: Yes, he trained his body with a boxing trainer and he could beat any normal player, like Lewis or Klitschko, in twenty to twenty-five moves.

Me: He'd get murdered in the ring.

RajKO: And don't forget, he gets a five-minute rest between boxing [while playing chess], so he could run.

Me: He'd get turned into a lot of lumps.

RajKO: I don't think so.

Oy. I could see Kasparov dead, showing up at St. Peter's gate, and St. Peter going, "Were you trying to kill yourself?" And Kasparov going, "I don't recall wanting to."

Against this backdrop, Woolgar stood out like Halle Berry at a fat farm. He was devoting his life to this. He was running five miles every day, followed by two hours in the gym and an hour of chess. He was pretty good at both. He'd better be. Two years of work were coming to a head very soon in one scary night.

Quiz:

Which strategies are boxing and which are chess?
  The LaBlanche Swing
  The Frisco Crouch
  The Texas Tommy
  The Philadelphia Shell
  The Spanish Exchange
  The Pin and the Fork
  The Indian
  The Turk

A: The first four are all boxing, the last four all chess.

Also: Somebody needs to make a chess boxing movie in which the bent-nose mafia mook comes into the pre-fight locker room and says to the fighter: "Listen up. Da boss wants you to go down in the fifth."

The terrified chess boxer argues, "No! I can't!"

"Yeah, you can," warns the mook. "Let him take yer queen. And no funny bizness, or you'll be movin' pawns witch yer elbows the rest of yer life!"

At last, the big night arrived—August 15, 2008—the first chess boxing card in British history. More than 150 people crowded into a place called the Bethnal Green Working Men's Club in East London, which isn't a strip joint but a kind of blue-collar nightclub. Inside was the largest paying audience for a chess match in the UK since Kramnik vs. Kasparov in London in 2000, even outselling—yes—the club's recent Mexican wrestling event.

You can see why. Ask your buddy if he wants to go to a chess match with you, he'll suddenly come down with mono or rickets or both. But if you mention that between the rapid-fire rounds of chess, there will also be people punching the mucus out of each other, plus a bar, followed by an after party, how's Mexican wrestling going to compete with that?

By dinnertime, Woolgar was as nervous as a quart of coffee. He was not only the promoter, manager, ticket agent, media director, and technical advisor, he was also half the main event in the heavyweight division. He'd sunk a silo of his own money into this. Worse, he was up against a brute with a broad back and long arms named Stewart Telford, who once owned a 5–5 record in amateur heavyweight bouts. Telford worked with juvenile offenders, so you got the feeling he'd be able to hold his own against a very polite, false-aged ex–BBC producer.

It was only a two-fight card. Sascha the Flascha opened against a fireplug Dutchman and didn't disappoint. Sascha took him out in the seventh round—on the chess board, no less—although it took the in-house bonehead commentator thirty seconds to realize Sascha had checkmated him. OK, so it's a new sport. We're still trying to iron the wrinkles out.

Eventually, it was time for the main event. Telford came out first in a Tyson-like black cape with two guys in white vests escorting him. He seemed to have hit a few too many donut shops on the way to work over the years, and immediately you could tell that Woolgar, who came out by himself to Guns N' Roses, was more fit.

First round is always chess, so the two gladiators went through the traditional donning of the . . . headphones? Yes, huge headphones to help them concentrate and avoid hearing advice yelled from the crowd. What was playing in the headphones? "Choral music, with sounds of the ocean," Woolgar said. Funny, I just can't see Mike Tyson listening to ocean sounds minutes before he fights, can you? *More theagullth, dammit!*

The two felt each other out on the chessboard for the first four minutes—each safely castling their kings away—with nothing much coming of it, and soon the bell rang and they removed the board, table, and two chairs from the ring in order to let the punching begin. The inebriated crowd was much louder than anybody would've thought. And perhaps spurred on by it, the two started brawling. All the caution and tiny steps on the chessboard were gone now, replaced by two palookas whaling at each other like Dublin bar patrons. Telford greeted Woolgar's face with a hook very early on, leaving him with a nice mouse above the eye. "He kept lining me up where the spotlights were blinding, then coming in with lightning-fast hooks to the temple," Woolgar recalled. "He caught me a couple of times and rocked me, but I managed to respond with a perfect right uppercut which landed on his jaw and made him think."

In Round Three, the best thinking on the chess side was done by Woolgar, who took charge of the middle and even captured a piece. It's a very odd thing to hear a lot of lusty Brits roar for a captured pawn.

When the two went back to the ring for Round Four, one could hear Woolgar's corner telling him to "Make him miss! Make him miss!" Woolgar heard and obeyed. "I just stayed slightly out of reach and watched various fists whizzing past my jaw but not connecting," Woolgar remembered. Maybe it was fear, but his leaden feet seemed to be lighter and he was no longer absorbing leather facials. By Round Five (chess), it was clear Woolgar was the Doberman and Telford the pork chop. He was starting to dominate the sixty-four squares. He looked in command of the whole night. Prepare the crown. But then, in Round Six, a very odd thing happened. Woolgar started listening to the suddenly bloodthirsty crowd.

"Fuck him up, Timmy!" somebody hollered.

"Knock his fucking head off!" another screamed.

You know how rowdy chess boxing crowds can get.

Somehow, Woolgar was flummoxed by it. He remembers thinking, "That's not the sort of thing I want to hear at my fight!" Although exactly what he was expecting them to yell, he had no idea. "Some sort of sporting soundtrack from an old Basil Rathbone movie perhaps," he says. "You know: 'Jolly good show! Oh I say, what a corker!' " And while he was wondering how his chess boxing event had turned into an NHL game, Telford planted a straight right-hand flush in his kisser. While Woolgar's head was snapping back, Telford added a fierce left hook on his temple for good measure. Woolgar started hugging Telford then like he was Bela Karolyi, hanging on for dear life. Soon as the ref separated them, another right hook came, which Woolgar ducked and followed with a combination to Telford's ribs. The bell rang. It was a great round and nobody could remember anything like it in Fischer vs. Spassky.

The doctor and the ref examined the swelling under Woolgar's eye, but let the bout continue. Which meant he had to go play chess with one eye, one glove, and a spinning brain. Luckily, Telford's mind was also moving at the speed of cold honey tipped over. The two of them made only three moves in four minutes. It was the Stupor Bowl. Perhaps even the ref was woozy, because he did nothing to speed them up. Suddenly, they were back in the ring, and this time Woolgar was on the counselor like freckles on Opie. He pummeled him in the corner, against the ropes, with his back to the lights, everything. The crowd was beside itself as the bell rang.

As they sat down for chess and Round Nine, Telford's brain must've been on sleep mode, because, by expert accounts, he played chess like a poodle on Xanax. "Twice in five moves he was oblivious to the long-range diagonal threat of the Black queen," RajKO wrote breathlessly of the match later. The second time, 2:23 into the round, Woolgar delivered checkmate.

All of which led to a deliriously happy chess boxer named Tim Woolgar accepting his honor as the Great Britain Chess Boxing Organization Heavyweight Champion of the World from Great Britain Chess Boxing Organization director Tim Woolgar. It was a very easy picture to take. One guy. Plus, nobody thought to make up a belt.

Telford admitted later that his strategy was to play chess slow and box fast. "He took some pretty clean, hard shots," Telford admitted. "He wobbled a few times, but didn't give up."

Satchel in the teeth, my friend. Satchel in the teeth.

· · ·

Overall, I believe chess boxing has a bright future, provided it adopts immediately and forthwith my list of improvements, which will take it to the upper stratospheres, or at least ESPN6:

- Make the chess harder by insisting the combatants play it with *both* gloves on.
- Between rounds, sexy librarian ring card girls should sashay around with their hair up, lensless glasses on, holding copies of Dostoyevsky over their heads, wearing cleavage-laden Swarthmore tops and short shorts with some kind of cheesy ad on the butt, such as, "You won't get rooked at Sam's!"
- The chessboards themselves should have little tiny boxing ropes around it. And be cleaned at least once a decade, for sure.

8

Drinking Games

(Note to the reader: As we researched this, we collected what we believe is a Guinness world record for euphemisms for "to regurgitate" or "regurgitation." Feel free to count along!)

This is about games in which people purposely drink vats of alcohol that would float the Queen Mary, often for the sole purpose of throwing up (1) in as multicolored a manner as possible. These are called drinking games. Believe me: Most of your tuition money goes to them.

This all started at a Fourth of July event near our home in Hermosa Beach, CA, called the 34th Annual Iron Man, which we naively thought might actually center on running and swimming and stopwatches. We were very mistaken.

At first, it *looked* like an actual athletic event. About 500 young men were there with their surfboards. But we also noticed they were all carrying six-packs, twelve-packs, even cases of beer. Seemed odd. We noticed those same guys burying their six-packs in the sand, or under their discarded shirts. Paranoid bunch, we thought.

We soon found out that the rules for this Iron Man were much different. The combatants had to paddle their boards a mile, yes, then ditch the boards on the beach and run a mile, yes, but the third leg required them to chug their warm six-packs of beer in twenty minutes or less without spewing (2) in order to post a time.

Of course, these are American young men, so 95 percent of them were in it purely for the yak-fest (3). In fact, many of them were ingesting colored Jell-O, half bottles of mustard, and food coloring, to give their hurl (4) a colorful aspect, like a colored mouth fountain (5). Some guys even ate sprinkles. Festive! We saw one man in a Speedo eating giant spoonfuls of peanut butter and honey just before the race was about to begin. Why? "Sticks on people better," he explained.

You tell me. How can this *not* be in the next Summer Games? Or at least the Blowlympics (6)?

Soon they were off, and I can honestly say I have not seen a bigger bunch of cheaters since the U.S. House of Representatives annual golf outing. Almost none of them paddled to the half-mile mark before turning around. Some of them barely went 300 yards. The running was even worse. A lot of those guys didn't even get 100 yards. One of the first guys in was a firefighter named Mike McIndoe.

"How'd you get done so fast?" I asked. "You've been training?"

"No, I didn't come close to running the mile," he said as he started to rip open his first beer, "and I cheated even worse on the paddle."

Yet the beer drinking is conducted under the strictest guidelines. There is a judge for every six iron men, weighing the cans when they're done to be sure they're empty, and using stopwatches to mark to the second when the sixth and final beer is drained. Mike was one of the first to finish, but soon after great multitudes finished. And that's when the first great beach retch (7) happened.

It was a young, skinny Asian guy. The volume, the power, and the arc of his heave (8) were chilling to behold. It went at least ten feet and yet never got wider than eight inches around. It resembled a New York City fire hydrant let loose. If I'm lying, I'll let him entertain at my daughter's wedding. It was a bit like witnessing a space launch, or some kind of Hollywood special effect. There is no way a human could project the contents of his stomach (9) with such astonishing violence and yet—dare I say it?—beauty. Were we in Salem, Mass., in the 1600s, he'd have been burned as a witch.

"Oh, my God!" TLC said, mouth open.

I advised her to keep it closed, lest he do it again.

This modern-day Horkules (10) was a University of California–Berkeley premed student named Brent (Hurtsauce) Yeung. Over the next twenty minutes, we saw this Duke of Yorking (11) do amazing things. For instance, even beforehand, he could pick out not just the poor unknowing bastard he was about to gak (12) upon, but where exactly he would hit them. "Fat guy," he would say. "Crotch." Next thing you know, some guy would be looking at his swimsuit in horror, then looking up to see Hurtsauce cackling.

"I didn't really know I had this talent until I came to this thing," recalled Hurtsauce. It was an amazing statement, like Van Gogh saying, "I didn't know I was artistic until somebody gave me a brush."

And as we watched him pukepaint (13) another poor soul from twelve feet away, I kept wondering what kind of doctor he was going to make.

Nurse: Dr. Yeung! Come quick! The ICU is on fire!
Dr. Yeung: Brrrrrraaaaaaaaaawwwwwwnnnnnggh!
Nurse: Thank God!!

All around us now, buff guys in swimsuits were standing in circles, waiting to see who was going to barf (14) on whom and with what style points. One guy would suddenly just lurch (15) and coat his buddy in innard juice (16). And the buddy would laugh hilariously and chug some more, hoping his innards would soon involuntarily fire back. And I was watching all this when it suddenly hit me. *Oh, shit. I'm standing in one of these circles!* And that's exactly when I looked up to see a man do a kind of Rainbird lawn sprinkler imitation, blowing chunks (17) in a 180-degree circle that got Yours Truly directly in the chest.

(Note to editors: I'm definitely going to need a bigger advance.)

I remember—as I was sprinting madly to the ocean—that it felt warm and surprisingly odor free. Sort of like having a baby throw up on you, only the baby is 180 pounds and has a goatee. My sprayer's name was Jason Norvelle, twenty-nine, a restaurant manager in Los Angeles. "Sorry, dude," he said, clasping my shoulder. "But it had to be done."

And I suppose he's right.

Just as this had to be done: *Jason Norvelle has sex with farm animals.*

The event on Hurlmosa Beach opened my eyes to a world of competitive drinking and Technicolor yawning (18) I never knew existed. And so I began collecting them. This was easily done during my work visits to America's college campuses, where these games seem to be more popular than sex and pizza combined.

And while I realize binge drinking on campus is a problem, I have to point out that not once did I see a single college kid participate in one of these games and then get behind a wheel. Most of them were in campus bars and just stumbled back to their dorm rooms, realized they were in the wrong one, and slept there anyway. Doesn't make it right, only makes it slightly less dumb.

Anyway, I have narrowed the best college drinking games to these:

Weakest Bladder

This was invented by a clever bar owner, but nobody can seem to remember which. There is a reason for that.

At 9 P.M., all bar doors are closed and guarded. The drinks then become free and remain free until the first person pees. Drink up, even guzzle if you want, but as soon as someone urinates, it's back to $5 beers and $11 martinis. Can you imagine the greeting the offending small-bladdered turncoat gets when he comes out of the restroom?

Damn, dude! You never heard of Flomax?!?

But I know a way to break the backs of these clever bar owners. It's called Stadium Pal. It's a device that allows you to pee into a catheter—the urine collecting in a plastic bag strapped to your leg—without anyone knowing but you and—if you screw up installing it—your dry cleaner. It was invented by a Philadelphia Eagles fan who didn't want to miss a play. I tried it at a Dodgers game and was able to drink eight beers over seven innings and never miss a—well, it's baseball, so nothing happened anyway—but still! At only $30, this thing could pay for itself in half a Weakest Bladder night!

Family Feud

Two teams of five guys each bring a thirty-pack. First team to finish wins, with one proviso: Each player can chunder (19) only once. If you do it twice, you're out. And this is what your average college guy thinks when he hears that rule: *You mean I get one free cookie toss (20)!?! Cool!* As in the Iron Man, the vomit (21) becomes a weapon, the more colorful, the more pointed, the better. My son, Jake, a graduate of the drinking-games capital of the world—the University of Wisconsin—says he has one friend who eats an entire Domino's pizza beforehand just to give his gak (22) real texture and flair.

Apple Ball

The competitors stand in a circle and bat around an apple. You can't catch it, only slap it toward one of the others. It's like pepper in baseball. If you let it drop or it gets by you, you must chug. If you chug three times, you must assume the position—hands and knees on the ground. Then the person who last touched it before you screwed up lines up and smashes the apple into your cranium, splattering it all over your forehead and the room.

You can only hope you are not playing with Roger Clemens.

I imagine a person who is very bad at Apple Ball could even get rather good at it, if he lived. "Oooh, that felt like a McIntosh, maybe three weeks picked? Not quite ready for pie, though."

The Ray Charles

Blindfolded, you throw three pennies at the bar. Whatever bottles you hit, that's in your shot. Not really a game, I guess, but I keep waiting for a guy to hit whisky, schnapps, and Windex.

Kings

This one is sinister. Everyone sits around a table with their drink. There is a deck of cards. Each card has a certain predescribed value. If you are dealt an ace, it might mean you must drink half of the beverage of the person on the left. A 3 might mean you can never say first names, under penalty of chugging. But a king? A king is nasty. When you get a king, the rest of the group gets to go into your cell phone and make you call anybody on your contacts list. Might be your alcoholic uncle. Might be a guy they know you owe money. Might be your ex. You must speak to that person for at least two minutes and—most importantly—cannot mention you are playing a game.

> *You: Uh, Amber? Yeah, it's Tom.*
> *Amber: Tom? What are you calling me for? I thought you said you needed space.*
> *You: Yeah, yeah, I do, I do. But I just, you know, needed to call.*
> *Amber: See, I knew this would happen! You still need me! I knew we couldn't stay broken up!*
> *You: No, no, we are! We ARE broken up!*
> *Amber: Then why are you calling me? Because you miss me! That's why! See! I knew it! I told my therapist—*
> *You: No! No! Seriously, we are totally over. It's just that I had to call—*
> *Amber: Oh! I knew we'd always be together! I knew it! I can't wait to tell Mr. Wiggles! And Midnight! Did I tell you Marshmallow came back? That's seventeen! All seventeen of my babies are back! Eighteen including you! Oh, I'm so—*
> *Click.*

Guess Who's Drinking?

Everybody gets clear water in their cup except one, who gets straight vodka. Everybody chugs. If anybody can tell it was you who had the vodka, you lose and must chug another. If someone accuses the wrong person, he loses and must chug. One flaw in the game: People get bored with being right and start guessing wrong on purpose, just to drink.

Eat Shit

You fill a simple one-pint beer glass with water and put it on the table. You float an empty shot glass in it. Competitors then try to bounce quarters into it. Each person gets ten shots—three points for getting the quarter into the shot glass, one for just getting it into the beer glass. If in ten shots you don't score any points at all, you must move away from the table, assume a push-up position, and eat something off the floor. And in college dorm rooms, that could be anything from a suspicious Vienna sausage to a moss-covered Cheeto. In fact, the item you eat might not even have been dropped there by the current residents. It could've been three renters back. Disgusting to you and me, Tuesday to drunk collegians.

"I've had to eat shit off a guy's floor before," one young man told me.

"Not too good at that game, huh?" I sympathized.

"Game?" he said.

Hockey

Somebody spills a drink and someone else hollers "Zamboni!" You must immediately stoop and suck all the beer up off the table. A very skilled player is apparently Tonya Harding.

Tourette's

Maybe my favorite. The usual setup: Table. People. Drinks. Before each person is dealt a card, he must declare what his Tourette's affliction is. In other words, he must declare what must be blurted out without thinking when the time comes. Some samples:

- Priest pick-up lines
- Porn names not currently in use
- Places you'd hate to own a time-share

Now the cards are flipped up one at a time to each person in turn. As soon as two cards match—say, you and your buddy, Tank, each get a 7—you must blurt out Tank's Tourette before he can blurt out yours. So if you holler: "Ready for the Second Coming?" before Tank hollers: "Fallujah!!!" then you win.

Ridiculously fun.

The Boot

Featured at Madison, Wisconsin's Essen Haus—one of the happiest places on earth—where half the restaurant is playing it at any time, including 11:45 A.M.

Delicious, frosty German beer is poured into two-liter glass boots and delivered to the table, where as many as twelve people sit thirstily. A live polka band plays. Huge plates of wienerschnitzel drift by. Buxom waitresses in St. Pauli Girl getups lean coquettishly forward without bending their knees. Many people have asked to be buried there.

The game begins with one person taking a huge chug of the boot and passing to the left. Each chugs, but takes care not to be the second-to-last chugger. If you are, you must buy the next boot ($20). So as you lift the great chalice to your lips, you think to yourself: *Do I chug this whole goddamn thing? If I don't, the next guy might! Or do I take a small sip and leave him with more than he might be able to chug? If I chug this whole goddamn thing, I will trig (23) worse than Linda Blair in* The Exorcist. *But if I take a small sip, I will be known across campus as the biggest pussy since Garfield.*

You're thinking all this as your whole table is pounding their open palms on it, trying to coerce you into chugging. In fact, sometimes the whole damn restaurant is pounding, especially for any competitor at the crucial to-sip-or-tip point. The crowd wants to see him chug and then chum (24). It takes a village to raise a ralph (25).

One night during our research, there was a table of eight guys near us playing Boot. One scholar was so hammered that nothing he was saying made any sense. He needed to buy a vowel. He was so near the gag (26) point, you could almost see the rouladen peeking up above his epiglottis. The boot came to him and it was at least half full. Keep in mind: that's more than a quart of beer. He set his jaw and locked his knees into a stand. The entire restaurant pounded. I slid my chair back five feet.

He raised the boot to his flush-red face, closed his eyes, took a deep sigh, and began chugging. And against all sense and logic, he did not stop until the glass boot was empty. He slammed it down and started to stagger away. His buddy to the left leapt up to try to hold him up. They instantly headed for the bathroom, hoping not to boot (27) the boot before they got there. The floor under him turned to a roiling sea. He took three steps sideways for every one he took forward. Somehow, he got all the way to the men's room. Its swinging door had not quite yet closed behind him when we heard the roar of his powerful egress (28). It sounded like a DC-10 engine firing up. Naturally, the crowd erupted in joy.

The buddy to his right—the one who was stuck buying the next boot—looked at me and declared, "That's called showing your tits."

It was very emotional.

Beer Pong

This is the most popular drinking game in college, by far. Some people call it Beirut. It's played on Ping-Pong tables, picnic tables, and, at med schools, operating tables. I've seen guys take the doors off their rooms and set them on two old kegs. It's played by teams of two. Ten cups—half-filled with beer—are set like bowling pins at each end. Each team takes turns trying to throw a Ping-Pong ball into the other team's cups. If they sink it, you must chug it. That's when an all-out Noonan breaks out. Guys begin doing the pogo stick, yelling unspeakables about your sister, and just generally acting like Alec Baldwin in custody court. First team to sink all ten cups wins.

I'm telling you, this could be the next poker. People get

addicted to it. People play it every night. But it all took a giant leap forward when TLC looked up from her laptop and said, "Did you know there's a World Series of Beer Pong? In Las Vegas? With a $50,000 first prize? And it's open to anybody?"

Lightbulb!

We knew we were in the right hotel when we saw a scruffy guy going up to his room with a box of two hundred Ping-Pong balls in one hand and a thirty-six-pack of Natural Light in the other. These guys were pros. One team—Smashing Time from Long Island, NY—had won nine different satellite tournaments. Both guys had quit their jobs just to play beer pong full time—in tournaments, in bar games, in money games. "We make about seventy percent of our shots," says Mike (Pop) Popielarski, twenty-five, of Massapequa, NY.

Wait. Seventy percent? Throwing a 2.7-gram ball into a four-inch-diameter cup from eight feet away, half crocked? That's like throwing your key card into your hotel-room door seven times out of ten. Try it tonight at home. If you make 30 percent over a full game, I'll tongue-bathe your cat.

The next day in the giant ballroom of the Flamingo Hotel there arrived 414 teams—most of them hungover twentysomething males, all of whom forgot to pack razors. There were maybe six female teams, and three of those were wearing ultra-hot pants and ultra-low-cut tops, the better to distract the guys with. I mean these shorts were *short*. I've seen doilies with more material.

Anything went. One team dressed as a sex-obsessed octogenarian couple. One guy would whip out his package as the other team shot. Guys would cabbage patch, moon, howl, clap, whistle, even rip off their shirts just as their opponent shot. It was all perfectly legal. It was even in the official rules: "No player may take offense to anything said or done during a game, even if it involves their mother."

The team names were good, too. There was:

Shortbus Superheros
Chase's Mom's ATM
White Men Can't Pong
Josh's Mom Is Dirtier and Sluttier Than Ever
My Couch Pulls Out but I Don't

The sentimental team was The Iron Wizard Coalition, mainly because they had been in the finals the year before, thought they'd sunk the winning cup with their opponents still four cups behind, and immediately went triple Grammatica, including falling on the floor in delirium. But the beauty of beer pong is the diabolical "rebuttal" rule, which states that the losing team gets one final chance to tie as long as they never miss again. Four cups in a row, under pressure? Impossible! Except that's exactly what LA's Chauffeuring the Fat Kid did, then won in overtime. It remains the Bobby Thomson home run of beer pong.

Second-place prize for the Wizards? Nothing. Beer pong is winner take all.

Ouch.

"I had that money spent," says Mike Hulse, twenty-eight, of the Wizards. Worse, less than a month later, his fiancée left him, sticking him with a $6,000 custom-made engagement ring he was able to sell for only $1,000. "Have I thought about last year?" Hulse said between games. "Every time I pay a bill. Every freakin' time."

There was one team there that was even older than me. Their best player was fifty-four. "I knew I was in trouble when I signed up online," the guy said. "The 'birth year' choices didn't go back far enough to my year. It only went back to 1960. I needed 1954." Cruel.

The rules allowed for teatotaling teams, too. Anybody could put water in their cups—if they could stand the verbal abuse they'd take for it—but we found the only team that did: Mrs. and Mrs. Lara and Kristin Mendez. That's not a misprint. They're a married lesbian couple from New York. "Our strategy was don't drink at all," Kristin said. "That way you'll have the advantage because you're sober. But we lost so much the first day, we gave that idea up. It just felt unnatural."

Just to recap: The lesbian married beer pong team hates anything unnatural.

My favorite team, though, was François the Butt Duster, mostly because they were my sons—Kel, twenty-three, and Jake, twenty-one. The name comes from my days going to the *Sports Illustrated* swimsuit shoots. There was a body-makeup man there we called François the Butt Duster. He was allowed into the dressing rooms and the tents with the naked supermodels because he was gay and French. He'd be in there with a stark-naked Heidi Klum or Elle McPherson, dusting their butts with his little French-maid feather duster, applying makeup, and cooing, "Oh-la-la, Tyra! Your bottumm—eet eez parfait!" Afterward, though, you'd always want to have beers with François because in actuality he was neither gay nor French. He was Frankie from Yonkers. "Cindy Crawford is hotter 'n the Fourth of July!" Frankie would say to his rapt audience. "Fuggedabouddit!"

Not since a Jose Canseco BBQ have you seen so many big guys and so many small balls. It was sloshy and loud and smelly everywhere you went. And all of it under fancy crystal chandeliers. It was a parent's hell. You half expected to have some mom come in, turn off the music, step to the mike, and go, "All right. You boys go outside and get some fresh air now. I need to vacuum."

The Butt Dusters started off white-hot—4–0—including a victory over a team from Rochester, which, no joke, would, just out of nowhere, slap each other in the face *hard*. The slapee, red-cheeked, would just look at his partner—stunned—and finally yell, "Yeahhh!!!" One team of women regularly flashed their chests to distract their opponents. But since that team went 1–11, you began to question their motives. Or the chests.

The Butt Dusters refused to be dragged down to the distracters' levels, though. In fact, when the other team threw, they wouldn't even watch. Not as a dis. They were just too nervous. They never thought they'd win even one game against the world's best, let alone the first four in a row. Jake kept taking fake texts the whole game. Kel kept turning away and pulling his shirt over his face. They eventually faded to a record of 7–5, just missing the third-day cut by one win, but seemed somewhat relieved. "I'm SO sick of beer," Kel said at the end.

Again, sentences you never thought you'd hear.

The star-crossed Iron Wizards finished forty-ninth, which left the final down to two teams who play out of Long Island, NY— maybe they should call it Pong Island?—both of which were so good and dispatched their opponents so quickly that they actually had to *sneak* beer just to slake their thirst. One was the aforementioned Smashing Time, two high school jock stars who stood six-six and six-four. "I just throw it like a free throw," Pops said. The other team was Getcha Popcorn Ready, whose players stood six-three and six foot. Leaning is legal in beer pong. Did you hear that, Yao Ming?

Perhaps worried about his thirst again, Smashing Time's Ron Hamilton, twenty-five, prepared for the final day by chugging a bottle of Jack Daniel's that morning. "The key for us today," he said, "was me getting really drunk."

Not the kind of quote that's going to get you on a Wheaties box.

Since Popcorn came up through the loser's bracket, they would need to win both games to be crowned King Pong. Smashing Time only had to win one. But Popcorn won the first game in a shocker. And that's when something happened I've never even *heard* of before.

The two teams made a secret deal. They agreed that whoever won would cut the losers a check for $3,000. Can you imagine Tiger Woods and Phil Mickelson stopping before the Masters play-off and going, "OK, whoever loses still gets to wear the green jacket for a week. Deal?"

Turned out to be a dumb move for Smashing Time, which proceeded to knock out their ten cups in twelve balls. That's some mad ponging. And that was it. The next thing you knew, they were taking a six-foot novelty check back to their room.

As for the future, WSOBP organizers think they'll have over 1,000 teams next year, a monster sponsorship deal, and possibly a TV slot.

And that's all great, I suppose, but I don't think it's truly going to be big without some kind of rule incorporating projectile sicking (29). Can't you see some guy going for the $50,000 win when he's suddenly plastered by a fire hose of haver (30)?

And the victim will only be able to wipe off his face and say, "Dr. Hurtsauce, I presume?"

9

Zorbing

I t's a proven fact that American lawyers take 87 percent of the fun out of everything.

This is why all the diving boards are gone from swimming pools and all the cool powder tree runs at ski areas are roped off and why hundreds of school districts have banned tag from school playgrounds because it's "dangerous" and causes "feelings of low self-esteem."

Aubrey: You're It!
Alex: I believe you know my attorney, Mr. Rothstein.

This is how we came to live in a country where a woman could be awarded $40,000 for hitting a golf ball that ricocheted off railroad tracks and hit her in the nose.

Can we all slap our foreheads in unison?

That's why you can't write a book in search of the dumbest sport in America, because dumb sports are usually risky sports and American insurance lawyers won't let you butter a roll without signing a release.

But New Zealand? Now, that's a whole 'nother story.

In New Zealand, the lawyers are all dead or fired or smoking kiwis, because there is no such thing as suing somebody for personal injury there. You can't do it. It's against the law.

So, if you want to hurl yourself off a 500-foot-high bridge tied only at your ankles while screaming "Ohsssssshiiiiiiiittttttt!" there are plenty of people who will take your money to let you do it.

Drooling, we headed to the Soul of Stupid Sports, the nation where the sports are dumber than Tori Spelling—wonderful, gorgeous, faultless New Zealand.

We started, as anyone would, with cave rafting.

I can hear you silently judging me already. *You didn't bungee? You pussed out on bungee? Isn't bungee like New Zealand's national sport?*

No, Mr. Negative. I'd already bungeed. Everybody bungees. Yes, it's stupid, but it's stupid the way those stupid plastic Crocs shoes are stupid. It's already been well documented. Besides, TLC was so worried about me bungee-ing that she kept sending me videos from the disasters page at bungeezone.com. There were dozens of the-cord-came-off-his-feet videos, and even more the-cord-snapped-in-half videos, a few did-her-head-just-hit-the-rock? videos and one he-was-given-the-eighty-meter-cord-for-the-sixty-meter-jump video. It did not make for comfortable pre-bungee viewing.

Besides, how dumb is cave rafting? Actually, the Legendary Blackwater Rafting Company of Waitomo called it "The Black Abyss Tour." When I showed up at check-in, employees with clipboards were coming up to me saying, "Are you the black abyss?" And I wanted to reply, "Well, my ex-wife thought so."

As for TLC, she touched the ice-cold wet suits they wanted us to keep on for five hours, heard how we'd be rappelling down an unlit hundred-foot hole, taking a zip cord down another hundred feet, jumping off a cliff into a fifty-degree underground river populated with blind eels, then float in inner tubes under the light of maggots (glowworms) and crawl through a fifty-foot-long mud tunnel, up two waterfalls, and finally out again, and said, "Uh, I'll be in the car, thanks."

Good call.

I guess I knew the Black Abyss was a poor choice on the order of anthrax cupcakes when I got to the bottom of the rappelling cave and saw a pile of animal bones in the light of my helmet lamp. I showed them to one of our guides, Parker, a tall twenty-five-year-old blue-eyed spelunking freak. "It happens," he said. "Dogs get down here and can't find a way out."

He said that "probably" wouldn't happen to us.

For fun, Parker goes exploring, alone, for days at a time, looking for undiscovered caves. He finally found one last year. He christened it *Who Needs Nipples?* because to get to it, he had to shimmy through a hole so tiny that it ripped both his nipples. Now *that's* a weekend!

There are times he enters some incredibly huge labyrinth of caves and doesn't come up for three or four days. "You can't leave anything down there, absolutely zero," Parker explained. "You even have to pack out your own poop in a poop bag." (*Poop Bag,* by the way, would be a good name for a fantasy football team.)

The whole day was misery. I envied TLC her sunshine and her book and her aboveground world. Apart from the times when we were allowed to just float in our tubes and stare up at the mysteriously glowing maggots, it was about as much fun as being massaged with No. 2 sandpaper. To keep my mind off my shivering body, I'd grill Parker on why the hell he did this bizarre thing for a living when it seems so ridiculously dangerous.

"But that's the thing!" he argued. "Anybody you talk to thinks the risk of caving is off the charts, crazy high. But in twenty-two years of running this tour, the most serious injury we've had is one broken pelvis. So the actual risk is really low. Rappelling is the same thing. Perceived danger: high. Actual: low. And yet, driving on New Zealand highways? Perceived: low. Actual: very high!"

This was a subject a guy could warm up to.

The girl in the marabou heels at the end of the bar? Perceived danger: low. Actual: high.

Toward the end, I started to lose it altogether. My teeth were chattering a symphony as I paddled and waded and crept from one more dank, narrow, lightless cave to an even danker, narrower, even more lightless cave—keeping my hands out of the water as instructed so the eels didn't think my fingers were food. I was tiptoeing around with my fingers in the air, like Liberace in a wet suit. After five hours, I came to sympathize with Gollum from *The Lord of the Rings*.

What does it want from us, precious? It wants us to wade through the freezing slime, does it, precious? And we paid $49.95 for this? Oh, we hates it, precious! We hates it!

At last we climbed up those two waterfalls and, like Tom Sawyer and Becky, spied our first glimpse of sunlight in what seemed like months. I half expected CNN to be waiting as we crawled out. But, as it turned out, the only injury we had all day was at the free soup and bagel afterward. A guy from Canada was so starved and freezing, he burned his hand trying to hurry up the toaster.

Bagel toasting? Perceived danger: low. Actual: high.

Cave rafting as something to do for fun? Perceived: high. Actual? Lower than eel turds.

We arrived in Queenstown, the Extreme Sports Capital of the World, to a macabre site.

Three stories below the balcony of the apartment we rented,

there was a funeral bouquet that marked the spot where, three nights before, a drunk young man had fallen off the roof, exactly above our apartment, trying to awaken a girl he'd met in a bar. Add to that the item in the paper about a parasailing instructor who wrecked into the lake the day before. An instructor! And the TV story about a rugby field at the end of a dirt runway at the Queenstown Airport. Several of the kicks had near misses with small planes. "Somebody's going to die soon," a neighbor said.

Queenstown: A Thousand Ways to Die.

In Queenstown, you can pay to bungee from a cliff, bungee from a bridge, bungee from a helicopter, ski from a helicopter, bungee from an airplane, parasail, parasail off a roof, bungee from a parasail, swing from one canyon wall to the other, snow luge, and land luge. You can hunt sharks, feed sharks, and swim with sharks. We rode on a 700-horsepower Jet-Ski boat (Jet Skis were invented here) down a narrow river, at times on no more than three inches of water, coming within a foot of rock canyon walls while spinning 540s. Queenstown mainlines thrills. We took a "flightseeing" trip in a little twin-engine that skimmed maybe 200 feet over 13,000-foot glaciers, then navigated a narrow fjord into Milford Sound on a runway no longer than a Hong Kong driveway.

All that was probably dumb. But none of them seemed dumber to us than Fly by Wire.

Fly by Wire involves strapping yourself into a rocket-plane contraption that looks like something Wile E. Coyote would've ordered from ACME. It's about ten feet long, bright red, with a big propeller at the back. You lie facedown on it, with your legs all the way back toward the propeller and your arms extended out in front of you so you look like Superman in a bad helmet. They belt you in and hook the plane up to a steel cable that hangs down from an even bigger cable, which bridges two sides of a 1,500-foot-wide canyon. That's it. It's like a gigantic swing set, except instead of a swing you're in your own mini-rocket. They tow you up, let you go, and for five minutes you fly around the canyon, steering this way and that as your stomach threatens to fall out of your mouth, though you're still not as scared as the poor people on the observation platform below, whose haircuts you buzz at ninety-one miles per hour. Very bad place to work if you're Shaquille O'Neal.

"Theoretically, nothing can go wrong," the bus driver said as he took us up a heart-in-throat road to the canyon. "You can't fly into the canyon wall and you can't fly into the floor."

To which I added, "No, we can't do anything wrong. But you guys could? Right? Like not hook the cable up right?"

"I guess," he said. "It's never happened."

I wanted to say, "Wrong, Bus Boy," because, one time, something did go very wrong.

Fly by Wire was born out of a dream. A Kiwi named Neil Harrap woke up, made a bunch of drawings, turned it over to some engineers, and had it built. Everything went fine until the day a Swedish woman got into it and was happily zipping all over the canyon when she suddenly hit the handrail of the observation platform, breaking her arm. Turns out the winch that towed her to the top had slipped two and a half meters, just enough to change "buzz over" into "buzz straight into." In America, she'd own Neil Harrap forever. He would cut her lawn and make her spritzers the rest of her days. But in New Zealand, the government paid for her medical bills and sent her on her way. *And yet she lived!*

Still, word got out about the wreck and tended to slow profits. Harrap took the idea to the U.S. instead, building three of them off I-35 in Fort Worth. He only had them open six weeks when nineteen inches of rain buried the whole site like Pompeii. Plan C: back to New Zealand, and Queenstown, where we found it.

Hoping he'd worked the bugs out, I climbed onto the liftoff platform. The guy running the whole thing, Darryn Tarkington, thirty-two, said that while I was in the air, he'd tell me what I was doing wrong via giant signs. Then he started holding them up to demonstrate:

Turn earlier
Turn later
Full power
Crap
Give up

I went second—right after a big, handsome, twenty-three-year-old kid from Melbourne. As he was getting out, elated, I was getting in, slightly panicked.

"You didn't sweat this thing all up, did you?" I kidded, starting to lie down, face-first, into the bizarre little plane.

"Nah," he said, "but I did piss myself."

Feeling weak in the knees, I was looking for a way out. I'd noticed small planes and choppers and even a biplane fly overhead. "I notice the planes coming by," I said to Darryn. "Aren't we kind of close to the airport?"

"Yeah, but this is controlled airspace," he said. "They need permission to fly over us."

"But what if they forget to ask?" I thought. "Wouldn't I still be dead?"

By then, Darryn was pointing out the red emergency stop button "in case anything goes wrong," and also the green button to request another minute at an extra $15. One minute for $15. You don't see prices like that this side of the Moonlight Bunny Ranch. For some reason, I kept thinking of that poor kid and the funeral bouquet, and I was laying 7-to-5 I'd hit the red button before I'd ever hit the green. I felt the winch start to tow me backwards up the hill, whether I was ready or not. "Say hello to the goat for me," Darryn said as he waved good-bye.

The goat?

Sure enough, a hundred feet below me there was a goat, nibbling at the cable as it winched me up. *Wait. The goat is eating the cable? What if he bites through it? Jane! Stop this crazy thing!*

Too late. I was at the top—about 250 feet above the platform—and it was time for me to gun the engine and start strafing and soaring, except I felt nauseous, tilted ninety degrees upside down like that, watching the damn goat nibbling at my mortality.

Just screw it, I said, and I squeezed hard on the gas lever, which not only released the towing cable but goosed the plane so hard my hand slipped off it, which meant now I was just free-falling toward the platform, fishtailing as I went past everybody, in much the same style as a drunk America West pilot. I was sure I saw Darryn reaching for the *Crap* sign. I regripped and pulled hard and went flying up to the other side of the canyon, turned hard to the left, and felt my stomach do the rhumba in the zero gravity that was created at the top of the arc. Suddenly, I had only one thought:

Thank you, Neil Harrap.

Fly by Wire is not just dumb and dangerous. It's dumb and dangerous and wonderful. It's like driving a go-cart in midair. I buzzed TLC and then I buzzed the goat and then soared toward the top of the canyon on the other side. Now I had the hang of it. I'd get to the apex, then bank hard as if I were in a Sopwith Camel, feel this amazing zero-gravity rush, and then come swooping down the other side like a hawk after a rabbit. I swooped up and down that canyon, left and right. It was like being on that giant swing set, only Godzilla is your dad, and he's gotten ahold of A-Rod's roid stash, and he's pushing you so hard from one side to the other you think you're going to bump your head on a Quantas flight.

There was a hiking trail along the ridge of one side of the canyon and I noticed a guy stopped, looking at me. I supposed he was a little shocked to suddenly see a man, strapped to a rocket, gunning right at him. I think it caused him to squeeze his raisins pretty tight.

When the fifteen-second warning buzzer sounded, I hit that green button like a heroin-addicted lab rat. And I kept pushing it. I would've spent a month's salary on that damn button if I could've, but you only get one push. Still, it's not often in life you suddenly get an extra minute after you thought you were done.

"I'd like a button like that," TLC observed afterward.

Funny girl.

After a while in Queenstown, you get so amped up doing all these adrenaline-rush sports that you start to lose a little perspective. For instance, there was this exchange in the apartment:

TLC: You want to take a swim?
Me: A swim?
TLC: Yes.
Me: And what, they pull you behind a cigarette boat or
what? You mean like an air swim? Like you dive off a cliff
and swim through the air until the cable catches you? Or
what?
TLC: No. (Pause.) Just a swim. In the pool. The swimming
pool.
Me: Ohhhh, right.

And then we found it. The Fort Knox of Dumb Sports, a place called The AgroDome, outside Rotorua, where they had more dumb sports than Liz Taylor has chins.

They had Shweeb. They had Swoop. They had Zorb. We had no idea yet what they were, but we knew we wanted them all. And it was odd to hear people's conversations near the ticket booth, as they contemplated which ticket packages to buy.

Kiwi A: Did you Shweeb?
Kiwi B: Nah, we just Zorbed. But we might Swoop.
Kiwi A: Yeah, I Shweebed and Swooped but haven't Zorbed.
Kiwi B: Well, I hear you definitely should Shweeb, Zorb, and
THEN Swoop, or you'll ralph.
Kiwi A: Got it.

. . .

We Swooped first, which exists in America under a dozen different names. You get bundled into a harness and towed backwards and up about 150 feet and then you pull your own release button, which sends you free-falling to your death, except that at about fifty feet, the cable catches hold and swings you to the other side, like a pendulum, where you go through the whole spleen-flipping process again. I asked the guys running it what kinds of odd things people scream as they're free-falling.

"The weirdest we've heard is, 'Holy Snapper Cow!' " said one of the guys. "Mostly, though, they just yell 'Assholes!' at us."

Sometimes, people get up to the top of the Swoop and can't get up the nerve to push the release button. They just flat-out can't make their hand do it. So they're just hanging up there, 150 feet above the ground.

So what do you do then?

"We go have lunch," he said.

(Actually, they have to ratchet them back down.)

Swoop: definitely not dumb enough.

Then we Shweebed. Shweeb is German for "float." And the slogan for the sport is "The Race Through Space." Another good slogan: "Shweeb—the Dumbest Thing Since Nehru Jackets."

A Shweeb is not the shortening of a "shitty dweeb." No, a Shweeb is a kind of recumbent bicycle inside a clear-plastic bean pod hanging from a 225-foot-long circular monorail. You get in it and pedal your way around the monorail for three minutes as fast as humanly possible, because you're racing the clock and another idiot riding a kind of recumbent bicycle inside a clear-plastic pod hanging from another monorail. That's Shweeb.

"It's going to be public transportation someday," beamed one of the shweebers running it. "They'll have these monorails all over the city and you'll just climb in and start pedaling anywhere you need to go."

Really? I said. *What if you're behind a really slow old lady assisted-living shweeber? How will you pass her?*

"Well," he said. "I don't know. But I know they'll be able to couple four and five shweeb capsules, like a train, for more power."

Really? I said. *But what if all five aren't going the same place?*

"Hmmm," he said. "I don't know. But someday they hope to get the speed up to seventy kmh. It'll be sweet-as [New Zealand for cool]."

Really? But how can that be, when the fastest speed Lance Armstrong can maintain for longer than twenty minutes is about 50 kmh?

"Lance who?"

Sigh.

We got in our pods, TLC in the left one and me in the right. It did look rather space-age, like something Captain Kirk might do in the exercise room on the U.S.S. *Enterprise*. There were seven gears to choose from and no brakes. You had handlebars, but it wasn't until later that I realized the handlebars were useless, since you don't have to steer when you're on a monorail. Where are you going to go, Auckland?

They reminded us we were being timed. They had the records of every nation posted. "Try to set your national record!" the kid told us. Yeah, right, coach.

With a bobsledlike push from the two shweebers, we pedaled our asses off for three minutes, our thighs burning by the time we finished. I did one minute and five seconds, and TLC did 1:10.

The one shweeber was tickled about TLC's time. Amazingly, she was only three seconds off the female American record. I was only five off the male. Wow! How cool is that? "Must be because we ride the recumbent exercise bike at home," I boasted.

"Yeah, you've probably built up the same muscles that you use here," the kid said.

In fact, I noted that TLC would've been the national record holder for Japan, China, South Africa, Germany, and Ireland. Holy Snapper Cow! Maybe this could be a whole new career for her! TLC, pro shweeber! Endorsements! *The Queen of Shweeba!* That kind of thing. I was pumped.

> Me: How many years has this thing been here?
> Kid: Years?
> Me: Yeah, how many years have people been coming and trying Shweeb and posting their times?
> Kid: Oh, we just opened three months ago.
> Me: Oh. OK. But, I mean, those records are for all the Shweeb tracks all over the world, right?
> Kid: Uh, no. This is the only Shweeb in the world.

OK, so maybe we table the whole career-change thing for now. All in all, I don't see Shweeb getting bigger than iPods in the U.S. In fact, I don't see them coming at all to the U.S., a nation with school gym classes that limit kids to "sports" like cup stacking, which is part of the reason that soon one out of every three kids will have obesity-caused diabetes.

> *Teacher: Uh, Justin, you want to go ahead and put down that chili cheese dog and Shweeb?*
> *Justin (mouth full): Wht z it?*
> *Teacher: You get into a clear-plastic pod hanging from a monorail . . .*
> *Justin: Yah?*
> *Teacher: And you pedal as fast as you can for three minutes!*
> *Justin (mouth fuller): I'll wt fr th vdo gm.*

Finally, and unforgettably, we Zorbed.

A Zorb is a giant eleven-foot inflatable plastic ball you climb inside and then try to hang on to as you get pushed down a mountain. It's just that stupid.

They throw a bucket of warm water inside so that you're slipping and sliding and flipping and flopping on the bottom half like a mackerel in the hold of a rollicking trawler. The ball spins *around* you as you tumble down the equivalent of a blue ski slope.

Of course, great zorbers don't put the water in. They try to run in it without falling as the Zorb rolls down the mountain. Only thirty-one people have ever done that. Only three have done that backwards. These kind of people call themselves "zorbonauts." These people do not have a lot to do.

Even dumber is "harness Zorbing," which is to strap yourself to the walls inside the Zorb and roll end over end until you chunder up the kraut dog you ate at a carnival in fourth grade. Ordinary people can try "harness Zorbing," though, unless it's windy, which it was on this day. Because there's no water in the Zorb then, the weight of the Zorb is too light and the wind can blow it a tad off course. One guy caught a gust, hopped the wooden retaining fence, and ended up in the parking lot. Another time a big wind blew a lady so hard down the mountain she hit the back wall, did a 360 inside the Zorb, and broke her ankle.

Did she sue for $100 million? Did she call her congressman? Did she write Gloria Allred? No! She went on with her life!

"We offered her a free ride," said the Zorb manager, Matt McLaughlin, "but for some reason she declined."

Could it possibly be that Zorbing was (gasp) *mostly safe*? "A few people lose their toenails once in a great while, but that's about it," Matt said.

When it was our turn, TLC and I got in a crappy brown van and rode to the top, where the driver got out, took one of the balls off the zorbulator (the conveyor belt that carries the Zorbs up the hill), rolled it onto a platform with a crossbar in front of it, stuck a garden hose in it for a few seconds, then made us literally *dive* through the thirty-inch-wide hole (not a sport for a rotund person—he'd wind up like Pooh in Rabbit's hole).

He looked in through the hole at us and said, "Everything box of fluffies?" (New Zealand for "Everything OK?")

"Huh?" we said.

Then he zipped the Zorb pod door shut and raised the crossbar. "Now stand up and start walking!" he hollered.

What? Push *ourselves* off the platform? Madness!

"Get up and start pushing!" he yelled again.

So we did. We got up and, like some kind of reverse Sisyphus, began propelling ourselves to our own literal downfall. Imagine!

Emergency-room doctor: So you were both zipped inside this giant rubber ball at the top of a mountain, right?
Us: Right.
Doctor: But you were on a flat spot. You were safe, right?
Us: Yes.
Doctor: And then you stood up inside the ball and began walking FORWARD? As in, OFF the mountain?
Us: Correct. How long in the casts?

Suddenly, we were over the precipice, flung backwards onto our butts and bouncing over, under, and through each other like dice in a cup.

Do you know how, in twenty minutes, you can go from not knowing a thing about a thing to that thing becoming one of the things you'll talk about the rest of your life? That's Zorbing.

Telling you, you must Zorb once. If you don't, that life will have been wasted. The feeling of having absolutely no control as you tumble like rag dolls in your own rubbery, watery, spinning, green-then-blue-then-green-again world is hilarious. It's like being on an extreme waterslide at a water park, only you have no idea where it's going, nor where you are, nor which way's up, nor when it will end. It's got to be the greatest invention since *Penthouse Forum*.

What's funny is that the Zorb was invented in the early 1990s for people to be able to walk across hot sand. It worked, but it wasn't exactly laughs. Then they thought it would be perfect as a way to walk on water. Also boring. Then some Kiwi said, "How about you get in it and I roll you down a hill?" Thus, Zorb history was made.

At the bottom, we caromed off a huge bank, through a giant grass curve, and then off another bank until the zorbanistas gained control of us, unzipped the pod hole, tilted the ball, and poured us out of the hole like huge, gloppy, fully grown babies. It was at that moment, as we were laughing hysterically, that I decided I *had* to bring the first Zorb franchise to America. After all, you can do it year round, you don't need much land, and there aren't many moving parts. Even our stupid lawyers would go for it.

"Do they pop much?" I asked Matt.

"Well, the plastic is three feet thick, so not really. All we do is give them a quick blow every morning and they're set." Well, who isn't?

"Do people ever get claustrophobic?"

"Sometimes. But I just zip them up and throw them down anyway. And they always end up thanking me afterward. They're always like, 'Man, that was the greatest time of my life!' "

"Much throwing up?"

"Not really," he said. "If they're gonna honk, they do it just before I close the hatch. I had an Asian kid the other day. I put him in at the top and he stuck his head back out and spewed all over me. So I hosed myself off and I said, 'You OK, then?' and he didn't say anything, so I zipped him up and threw him down. And he had the greatest time!"

I was really starting to like the way this guy talked. *Hell, yeah! You're gonna honk? I'm gonna zip you up and throw you down, cowboy! Sweet-as!*

I asked about buying a zorb. I'm figuring a sledding hill, a crappy van, a Zorb, a zorbulator, a few zorbanistas, a box of T-shirts, I'm going to make millions!

"They're about $11,000 U.S., but you can't buy one. You can only buy a franchise."

"But there's none in the U.S. yet, right?"

"Yes, there is one. Pigeon Forge, Tennessee, I think."

Rats! Figures. Pigeon Forge is the home of Dolly Parton. Hasn't she got enough giant, round, inflatable balls?

10

Baseball

f all the bizarre, senseless, and anvil-brained sports I dove into, the dumbest one was right in front of me—baseball. It's OK, I guess. It's just that not enough baseball players are swallowed up in tragic sinkhole accidents.

I suppose there was a time for it once, when people whittled and waited for the movie to change at the Bijou. But, like leeching, those days are happily gone and the truth has been revealed: Baseball is so crushingly boring you would sooner stick forks in your eyes than see another zoom shot of Andy Pettitte's nostrils.

I've heard all the arguments from seamheads: "It's a sophisticated taste. It's subtle. It's a game of patience and grace and strategy. We wouldn't expect one-celled organisms such as yourself to understand." If baseball is so subtle and graceful, how come the guys in the bullpen never watch it? They're either trying to spit tobacco juice onto each other's socks (very subtle) or figuring out how they can get Chinese food delivered.

No, there are at least 5,003 reasons to hate baseball, but I was able to reduce them to these seven:

1. Baseball is duller than Amish porn.

Name another sport that needs a seventh-inning stretch. Nobody gets drowsy watching football. It's my pet peeve: In baseball, an at-bat takes just slightly longer than the Crimean War. For some reason, after a pitch, baseball hitters take thirty-seven minutes to get back in the batter's box. They adjust their helmet, their jersey, their wristbands. They must re-Velcro their already-perfectly-Velcroed batting gloves. They adjust their belt, smooth their pantslegs, kick imaginary dirt off their cleats. And this is after they've let the ball go past. If they have swung and missed, they must actually unbutton their pants, take out their cups, blow-dry them, and put them back in.

And that's just the hitters. Pitchers fuss with their rosin bags, the rubber under their feet, and the brim of their caps, where the Vaseline is hidden. Then they stare in forever at the catcher's sign as though—if they wait long enough—the catcher might suddenly become Salma Hayek. Then they take a big, deep breath, stare over at third for a bit, go into a windup that would make a glockenspiel jealous, and then . . . throw over to first. Eleven times. By the time the pitch finally gets delivered, the 490-pound umpire has expired. I once timed the actual action of a three-and-a-half-hour baseball game: less than seventeen minutes. This is why—no lie—many people bring a good book to the game. See it all the time.

Seamheads argue that baseball is the only game that does not use a clock. Exactly. This is why any American under the age of twenty-five cares as much about baseball as a goiter seminar. If baseball did use, say, a fifteen-second clock between pitches, the game would be over in less than two hours and then World Series games wouldn't end as milk is being delivered to your home. As it stands now, baseball is as dead to your average nine-year-old as pogs. Baseball long ago lost the next generation.

Another thing: Why do relief pitchers need two minutes to warm up? They've been warming up! For ten minutes in the bullpen! Do substitute QBs get to warm up once they go in? Backup goalies? Can a 3-point shooter in a basketball game take eight or ten shots before we restart the game? No! While we're young, if you don't mind!

Attendance, amazingly, is still strong for baseball, and I know why. People don't go to baseball games to watch the games. Do you honestly think anybody cares how the Kansas City Royals do against the Cleveland Indians in July? No, people go to sit in the sun, eat foot-long hot dogs, visit, drink kiddie pools of beer, and stand behind home plate, waving their cell phone at the camera, screaming, "D'you see me? Do you? It's pointed right at me!" These last kind of people need to be tied to the 4:55 out of Buffalo.

For a time, there was a surge in attendance at San Francisco Giants games, but it turned out people were coming purely for the excellent and free wireless service at the games. This is true. You'd look up in left field and see women in spectacles downloading albums, hoping a foul ball might hit them so they might sue.

2. Baseball players are dumber than toe lint.

Baseball players are so dense light bends around them. They are the thickest of all professional athletes by a par 5, mostly because they usually leave for the minors before graduating high school and then spend nine months a year for the next twenty years with other baseball players, most of whom have read nothing longer than the Betty and Veronica Super Double Bubble issue. In 2004, Chicago Cubs pitcher Mark Prior gave the commencement address at the USC School of Business. The dean introduced him as one of only seventeen major leaguers with a college degree. Seventeen out of 7,500 players. Baseball must be very proud. That's almost what they have in the Jiffy Lube organization.

Baseball's tradition is to mock the intelligent player—"What are you, some kinda commie?"—and exult the bonehead. The dumbest players are the most fondly remembered. Recall Yogi Berra's classic: "You gotta go to your friend's funerals or they're not gonna come to yours!" Remember Dizzy Dean, after getting hit in the head? "Doctors examined Dean's head. They found nothing." Remember the Atlanta Braves pitcher who had to miss a start after suffering a burned stomach from ironing his shirt—while it was still on him?

I just usually pick out one player as an example of the kind of typical brainpower we're talking about: Gary Sheffield. Besides wearing out the patience of seven teams, this is a man who once:

- admitted he purposely threw balls over the first baseman's head and into the stands to punish his own Milwaukee Brewers fans for booing him. And why were they booing him? Because he seemed to purposely throw balls over the first baseman's head.
- said his uncle, Dwight Gooden, was justified in hitting his girlfriend.
- allegedly left two 9mm Luger bullets and threatening notes on the doorstep of the mother of one of his seven children.
- asked to be traded from the Dodgers because they were spending their money stupidly. Why were people accusing the Dodgers of spending their money stupidly? Because they signed Sheffield.
- refused to play in the World Baseball Classic because he wasn't being paid.
- borrowed steroid cream from Barry Bonds.
- contended that there are more Latin players than blacks in baseball because Latins are "easier to control . . . They have more to lose than we do. You can send

them back . . . You can't send us back. We're already here."

In Sheffield's case, that's exactly the problem.

3. Writers somehow think baseball is male childbirth.

There's no bigger gap in any sport than the one between misty-eyed Jack Kerouac–quoting baseball writers and red-eyed Jack Daniel's–drinking baseball players. Press-box poets like George Will are always waxing nostalgic about the game; everything is roses and sepia tones and tearstained "catches" with Dad. They'll see some rookie standing with some old vet in the outfield and say, "Imagine the lessons being handed down." And having been around the game my whole life, having played it, I can tell you the lessons. The old vet is saying, "You see the blonde with the rack sitting behind the dugout? She likes power tools."

4. Baseball rules are asinine.

In baseball, it takes only three strikes and you're out, whereas it takes four balls for a walk. This is why the very best hitters fail two times out of three, making baseball mostly all about disappointment. There is nothing in life more boring than a one-hitter.

If a ball hits the foul pole, it's fair.

In the National League, there is no designated-hitter rule, which means fans get the thrill of seeing a pitcher swing a bat at a ball the way Paris Hilton swings a shoe at a moth.

The infield fly rule states that—aww, forget it. It's understood by only three people—two of them in China. It's nearly as incomprehensible as the balk rule, which is simple compared to the rule that forces fans to wait up to three hours in the rain before the home manager has to call the game a rainout, thus allowing his owner to sell three more hours' worth of those little ice cream helmets while people wait. Bastards.

That is why I've developed my own new set of baseball rules, effective beginning tonight at midnight:

a. If you're 0-for-4 for the day, you no longer get to pick your own at-bat music. The crowd picks it for you. Is it our fault they choose "Tiny Dancer"?

b. You have fifteen seconds to get back in the box or back on the mound. If you're late, we bring out John Rocker to throw fastballs at your groin.

c. Three balls for a walk.

d. Every home run gets you an extra out.

e. Two outfielders.

f. If you're the dweeb on the cell phone waving at the camera, the rest of the people in your section get to pour Budweiser down your pants.

g. Any baseball player who wants to renegotiate his deal upward can do so. But that automatically clears the way for his mortgage company, his agent, and his ex-wife to renegotiate their deals up, too.

h. Every player will hang around for five minutes after batting practice and sign autographs before going into the clubhouse. This is not an original idea. One time, the Chicago White Sox tried to make it a club policy and Frank Thomas pitched a XXXL fit. "We have schedules," he said.

Oh, please. I've been with Frank Thomas before games. Here is his unbendable and demanding schedule for a 7:30 P.M. start:

4:30: Arrive ballpark.

4:45 to 5:15: Sit on huge leather couch in clubhouse, looking at porn mags and shooting breeze with other players.

5:15 to 5:30: Go into trainer's room and shoot breeze in there.

5:30 to 6:30: Take batting practice for fifteen minutes and then hang around the outfield shooting breeze and, if it's convenient, catching the occasional fly ball.

6:30 to 7:00: Go back into clubhouse, get dressed, sit on huge, black leather couch, and shoot whatever possible breeze has not yet been shot.

7:00 to 7:15: Throw away fan mail.

7:15 to 7:30: Get dressed.

So, Frank, you think you could spare five out of that?

5. Baseball has more unwritten rules than the Ming Dynasty.

Just a few:

- Forget what the rule book says about "knees to the letters," the strike zone is an inch above the belt to the bottom of the knees. In the National League, it's even lower than that.

- The second baseman does not have to touch the bag on a double play. Also, the first baseman can yank his foot off the bag if it's only a fraction of a second. Apparently, it's like one of those MapQuest pins. Anywhere in the vicinity is good enough.

- If you celebrate even a tiny bit at home plate after hitting a home run, we will throw a ninety-mile-per-hour fastball at the head of your team's next batter. The hitter is supposed to bury his eyes into the ground and run the bases as though he was on a run with General Patton. This has been going on for decades, but it was particularly stupid in the 2009 World Baseball Classic. The Netherlands was beating the U.S.A. when a nobody named Brian Englehart hit a dinger and apparently took one crow hop too many watching it fly out of the yard—perhaps because it was the first Dutch home run in WBC history and the greatest moment in Englehart's life. The American team decided he'd disrespected them. Decided he'd cleaned his toes with the American flag. Naturally, they threw the next pitch at the following hitter's earhole. This has killed people before, by the way, and blinded a couple others. A brawl nearly ensued, which would've been interesting, since the entire Dutch team was on speed skates.

This is typical baseball crud. Take the New York Yankees' emotional and big-hearted pitcher, Joba Chamberlain. He got a big strikeout in Cleveland one night and indulged himself in a joyous fist pump, à la Tiger Woods. You'd have thought he'd shot the White House dog. Yankees Hall of Famer Goose Gossage sniffed: "There's no place for it . . . That's just not the Yankee way. Let everyone else do that stuff, but not a Yankee."

Can you imagine this in any other sport? *After Woods made a huge putt on 13 and celebrated, Mickelson hit a retaliatory driver directly into Woods's stomach.*

• Players like Gossage get into the Hall of Fame if they moan long enough. For nine voting years, he and his 3.01 ERA weren't good enough—and they weren't—and suddenly, just like that, they were. Jim Rice wasn't good enough for fifteen years, and suddenly he was. In baseball, the whiney wheel gets the plaque.

• No media type may ask any manager or player an honest question. It must be couched in globs of puffery and doublespeak. For instance, if the Megaliths' first baseman boots an easy grounder to lose the game in the bottom of the ninth, the last thing a writer can say to the alcoholic manager is, "What happened at first?"

He'd get a snap of the neck, a bulled chest, and a screaming, "What happened at first? What kind of bullshit question is that? What did you think happened at first? Get the fuck out is what happened! Get the fuck out of my office!"

No, there has to be a long period of brooding silence—even though the room is full of reporters on deadline—and finally the senior newspaper beat guy is supposed to clear his throat and say, at last, "Brutal hop at first base, Skip. Just brutal."

And the manager is supposed to digest that for a minute, pull his hat back a little, and go, "Ahh, I couldn't see it. Hell, I thought the boys played their dicks off. What are you gonna do?"

One time, I purposely broke this rule, just to see what would happen. It was before an All-Star game, and Frank Robinson was an assistant coach for the American League. The Oakland A's' Jose Canseco was on the team and he was the most controversial figure in the game—sleeping with Madonna, looking like the roided-up Godzilla that he was, having balls bounce off his head and over the fence—so I said to Robinson, "What do you think of Jose Canseco?"

And he turned to me with eyes big as coconuts and a vein in his neck started throbbing and he said, "What do I think of Jose Canseco? WHAT DO I THINK OF JOSE CANSECO? Take a hike. Take a motherfucking hike."

Swear to God.

One day a few years ago, Cincinnati Reds starter Kent Mercker was knocked out of the box in a loss to the Mets. When reporters arrived at his locker, there hung this note:

"I waited fifteen minutes and had to go. I would like to answer any question with the standard good-guy answer:

1. Bad location with fastball
2. Fell behind too many hitters.
3. (bleep)ed
4. (bleed)ed
5. (bleep)ed again."

I always felt like Mercker hit on a very good idea there.
Since the whole give-and-take between
players/managers and the baseball media is such bull,
"standard answers" could save everybody a lot of time.
Why should reporters go to a locker to take notes when
they can go there to *read* one.

When the cleanup man strikes out five times in a
crucial pennant-stretch game, he could simply leave this
note:

1. Real nice park. When do the motocross guys get it back?
2. Yeah, well, you'd go oh-for-five, too, if you had Sarah
   Jessica Parker hitting behind you. No wonder I never see
   a damn decent pitch.
3. I told you. I'm not in a slump, I'm just hitting shitty.
4. Screw these fans. Does this town even HAVE an
   orthodontist?
5. (Bleep) their (bleep)ing shift.

And since a lot of baseball players have the moral
compass of AIG and often find themselves a little
sideways with the gendarmes, they could simply leave the
standard "bad guy" answers on a note at the sergeant's
desk at police headquarters:

1. Hey, I only punched the cop because he disrespected:
   a. me
   b. my peeps
   c. my new Suburban

2. It was profiling. They just think anybody doing 110 is *automatically* causing trouble!
3. I wasn't drunk. Those parked cars sideswiped *me*!

Someday, I may even try it. I'll leave the press box early for the local adult-beverage dispensary, simply pinning a note to the pitcher's locker with my standard questions and a blank for his answers:

1. The one Pujols hit off your forehead, did that hurt?
2. Do you think the eight walks in the third inning hurt your cause?
3. Where exactly should I go on my motherfucking hike?

6. The players cheat.

This is not news. It's like saying, "Wolves like meat." We all know it now: Many, if not most, baseball players cheated in some fashion in the Small Testicles Era, 1985–2005.

But unlike the Dead Ball Era, the Whites-Only Era, and the High Mound Era, the Small Testicles Era didn't apply to every player across the board. There was nothing Lou Gehrig could do to face black pitchers. It's not like he could suddenly sign with the Baltimore Black Sox. He was stuck playing a less-than-what-it-could-have-been game. It wasn't Denny McLain's fault he pitched in the High Mound Era. Every mound in the league was like that. But Derek Jeter competed against and faced teams full of juicers every game and he says he was on nothing. "I hear people say 'Everybody was doing it,' " Jeter said in the aftermath of teammate Alex Rodriguez admitting he binged on the syringe. "No, that's not true. Everybody wasn't doing it."

That's why I've never stopped pounding on the seamheads to keep Bonds, Clemens, Palmeiro, Sosa, and all the other cheaters out of the Hall of Fame. That's why I believe baseball should do what the Olympics do. When a player is caught cheating, his records from that year should be expunged from the record books, never happened, Wite-Out, like a Russian czar who suddenly never existed.

So why should all these phony career records be allowed to stay in the record book, with no asterisks? Because we need little tiny syringes next to them, that's why. Much more effective.

7. Most of the ballparks are precious enough to make your teeth ache.

Sometime in the last twenty years, baseball parks became some kind of Knott's Berry Farm attraction: Centerfields that rise suddenly for no reason (Houston). Fences that are eight feet high and then, a foot to the right, thirty-five feet high (Florida). Unneeded pylons that pretend to support your outfield fence (Arlington).

There was a time when ballparks were shoehorned into odd places and *needed* centerfields that rose (Crosley), green monsters that jutted (Fenway), simply because there wasn't enough land. But now it's just faux charm, like a waiter in some Vegas jousting restaurant going, "And perchance Milady would be pleased with Bac*O's?" What these new architects don't get is, those places were not all that charming in the first place. Guys broke their leg on that stupid rise in centerfield. Pitching careers were ruined in Boston. *Hey, I know! Let's bring back polio!*

It was all right at first. Camden Yards was pretty cool with the old train building behind right field. Coors Field had a nice nostalgia to it, I suppose, with all its exposed iron beams and old-timey scoreboards. And SkyDome, in Toronto, with its hotel rooms overlooking centerfield—well, how can you argue with a place that allows you to watch a game and people screw at the same time?

But then it all got so terminally cute. The swimming pool in right field at Chase Field in Phoenix. Really? A swimming pool? There's no swimming in baseball! Maybe all the architects can go drown themselves in it. And did Houston's Minute Maid Park really want to put an outfield flagpole in play? Did they really mean to re-create the old monument feel of Yankee Stadium when guys had to find balls behind the Babe Ruth monument and relay it back to the infield? It was stupid then. It's stupider now. Oh—and get this—it has a train that runs along the top of the stadium. Why the train? Who the train? What the train?

Consider San Francisco's Whatever Park (three names in its first six years). Its outfield wall is made of four (4!) different substances: everything from brick here to Cyclone fence there to, I don't know, Velveeta over there. An outfielder could get a facial tic trying to figure out how a ball is going to bounce. It also has a myriad of different heights, giving it more angles than Bernie Madoff. What is this, pachinko?

"People talk about the seventies and the cookie-cutter ballparks," says Todd Belzag, a statistician with Elias Sports, "and they go, 'What the hell were we thinking?' Well, I think we'll look back twenty years from now and go, 'What the hell were we thinking? Why were we putting this hill in centerfield?' I mean, in Fenway, they couldn't afford the street behind so they put the wall up in left. But don't tell me they can't afford it now." Exactly. In other words: Don't piss in my ear and call it rain.

I think we'll look back twenty years from now and go, "Can you believe, at one time, baseball was more popular than pro bass fishing?"

Me, I'll take football. The best player in football history was Jim Brown, a granite pillar of a man. The best player in baseball history was Babe Ruth, a Jell-O parfait of a man. The best arm in football was John Elway's. The best arm in baseball was John Elway's.

Football has cheerleaders. Baseball has batboys. Football has Tom Brady. Baseball has Don Zimmer. In uniform, no less. Football has Commissioner Roger Goodell, handsome, rugged, and sturdy. Baseball has Commissioner Bud Selig, who looks like a flu-ridden CPA who won some kind of contest to get on the field.

In football, an upset means something. The worst team beats the best team maybe once in twenty-five tries. In baseball, the worst team beats the best team two out of five. What's to celebrate? Fans get so excited in football they tear down the goalposts. Fans get so excited in baseball they sometimes look up from their BlackBerrys.

If you're at a football game, there are eleven different matchups you can watch on every play. Set your binoculars on the wide receiver trying to juke the cornerback or the center trying to bull the noseguard. In baseball, try setting your binoculars on anybody other than the pitcher or the batter.

Fan #1: Hey, what did the rightfielder do that time?
Fan #2: Well, first he put his glove on his knee, then he bent over, then he stood up straight again. Then he spat. Just like last time.

Football players come off the practice field looking as if somebody had used their helmets to boil lobsters. Baseball is so taxing that sometimes guys can get in only 18 holes before a game.

So let's call baseball what it is—a nap aid. And the next time somebody tries to make you feel guilty about hating baseball, remind him what ESPN college football commentator Beano Cook said when Commissioner Bowie Kuhn announced that the freed U.S hostages from Iran would all receive free lifetime baseball passes:

"Haven't they suffered enough?"

¶¶

Nude Bicycling

hen I got into journalism, I dreamed of winning Pulitzer Prizes, sending off breathless dispatches to a waiting nation, and meeting scar-faced sources who carried Glocks in their trench coats.

Never once did I think I would spend much of my time interviewing hairy, naked men. In over thirty-two years in this business, I have unwillingly conversed with more naked men than Jenna Jamison and the National Association of Proctologists, combined.

As a boy, I did not anticipate interviewing Yankee slugger Jason Giambi as he mindlessly cupped, adjusted, and recupped the only piece of clothing he often wore in the clubhouse, his lucky gold lamé thong.

I did not know that I'd one day spin out of my kneeling position at one New York Jets' locker and turn straight into Kimo Von Oelhoffen's ass.

I did not know I'd be riding along in a van, laptop open, interviewing golfer John Daly, only to look up and see him holding his—*quel est le mot juste?*—Big Bertha in his hand, laughing hysterically, displaying it like a Hebrew National kielbasa on *The Price Is Right,* and cackling, "This is why they call me Long John Daly!"

(And, if I may opine, rightly so.)

Sometimes it was worse than just naked. I'll never forget when I was twenty-five, having to interview legendary Indiana basketball coach Bobby Knight over breakfast at the Denver Tech Center Marriott. Except Knight didn't show up for breakfast. After waiting a half hour in the coffee shop, I managed to con a bellhop out of his room number, went there, and was greeted by a sliver of Knight, three-quarters asleep, through the four-inch gap he'd opened. "Coach Knight?" I stammered. "We were supposed to do an interview at eight?"

Grumble, hiss, grumble.

Finally, the door opened. I was greeted by the great man's bare ass as he turned into the bathroom and turned on the shower. "Make it fast," he growled.

Apparently, I was to interview him in the shower.

I did.

It got worse. After the too-revealing shower interview, the toweling off interview, and the brushing of teeth interview, Knight shoved the bathroom door in my face so that he could take his morning constitutional. He left the door open a few inches and said, "What else you got?" Apparently, I was about to do a Man on the Seat interview.

"Uh, well," I stammered into that awful cavern. "Do you, uh, do you ever see yourself coaching in the NBA?"

And as he proceeded with his morning duty, he said: "No, I don't think so. See, I'm a guy who enjoys working with the younnnnnnnggggggerrrrr type player, who—mmmggghh—still wants to learn somethinnnnnng about the game."

Therapy has not eased the pain.

I have done so much of this type of reporting, I have formulated my Four Rules for Speaking to a Naked Man:

1. Don't acknowledge it. If you acknowledge it or mention it in any way, you're gay. If *they* mention it, it's funny, and you're still gay.

During his unforgettable play-off run in 2004, Boston Red Sox slugger David Ortiz hit yet another crucial home run to win a monstrously huge game. There must've been a hundred of us waiting at his locker afterward. The hulking Ortiz came out of the shower and began wading through the sea of humanity, wearing only a towel and a scowl. Suddenly, he stopped, spun around, looked down on this tiny, middle-aged, bald radio guy, leaned over him menacingly, and growled, "Did you just look at my NIPPLES?!?"

The little guy was frozen with fear. He gulped for air and finally squeaked, "No."

Ortiz suddenly broke into a huge grin, slapped the little man on the back, and said, "Why not?"

2. Always write on a legal pad. The pad is your friend. It serves as a barrier between you and "it." "It" moves, the pad moves. Under no circumstances do you want to see "it," even out of curiosity, even accidentally. Things get destroyed, like your self-esteem. Most of these guys have units that could serve as LAPD battering rams.

3. Be alert. Just because they're nude doesn't mean they're neutered. I once interviewed Pete Rose across a shower curtain in the Cincinnati Reds manager's office in 1985, as he chased Ty Cobb's hit record. I was asking him, as he lathered, how much he lost at the horse track that year. There was a pause in the steamy room. Then he suddenly began yelling, "You can't crucify Pete Rose!" And then he threw his shampoo bottle at me. This is why the built-in sham-

poo wall dispensers of today are such wonderful inventions, in my opinion.

4. It's your job. Get over it. You want an interview, you've got to be OK with talking to guys with taco bits stuck in their junk. This is how they are. They're used to constant nudity, like nurses or masseuses or White House interns.

Some guys refuse to be interviewed naked, such as Kobe Bryant, Michael Jordan—who wouldn't even come to his locker until his tie was knotted—and former running back Eddie George. "I never felt like it was appropriate," George says. "Now, maybe if I was endowed like some guys I've seen, I'd come out stark naked, put my knee up on a table, face the crowd, and go, 'OK, who's first?' "

Other guys seem to relish it, like Johnny Damon of the New York Yankees. I'm still not sure I've ever seen Damon clothed in a clubhouse. The man is naked more often than the David.

You might think, "What a great job for a female reporter!" but you would be wrong. It's without doubt the hardest part of the job for women sportswriters. Most pro athletes are just slightly right of Charlton Heston and believe women have no right to be in a locker room at all. The rest just act like the cast of *Porky's 6*.

One of my friends was one of the first female American sportswriters—Betty Cuniberti of the *Washington Post*. One night early on, she was covering the Yankees and reportedly entered the clubhouse to find one of the team's stars, buck naked, swinging his schlong like a lariat and cackling, "Hey, Betty, know what this is?"

To which Betty—wonderful, unflappable Betty—answered, "Well, if it were bigger, I'd say it was a penis."

Former Washington Redskins lineman Dave Butz once told then–*Washington Post* writer Christine Brennan that if reporters were going to interview him while he was naked, then they should be naked, too, including her. Tit for tat, as it were. He probably had a point, but that policy could get awkward.

Me: Do you feel like your problem with free throws comes from
   the broken right wrist you had when you were eleven?
Shaq: . . . (wheeze) . . . (snort) . . . (cackle) . . .
Me: Look, if you're just going to laugh the whole time, let's just
   forget the whole thing!

But that got me to thinking, What if everybody in a sport WERE naked? The whole time—before, during, and after? The competitors, the refs, the hot dog vendors, Bud Selig, everybody? After all, the world's first organized sporting competition—the Greek Olympics—were conducted in the nude. What happened to that? Why couldn't there be an all-nude sports?

I was about to find out why not.

There are thousands of all-nude competitions all over the world, but most of them are "naturist" colonies, which seemed to violate our vague and very self-serving rules of the quest, one of which was that anybody could try to qualify for it. Besides, I once did a column on a nudist colony just north of Tampa and I have seen naked tennis. It is not pretty. While serving, there's no place to stick the second ball. And you are constantly hoping the winner doesn't jump the net to shake hands.

TLC found a man called The Ancient Brit, who had made it his life's goal to climb all the Scottish peaks over three thousand feet, nude. I figure the low altitude is to ensure against frostbite. He's also led nude kayaking trips and camping adventures. He offered to lead us on any sort of nature trek, sport, or climb, complete with any pictures we wanted, as long as we were both nude. "Really," he wrote, "I've got no problems with you taking pictures of me naked. No problem at all." And he attached about fifty pictures of himself, which, when we opened them, made us gasp.

The man was hung like a Clydesdale. Honestly, it was a baby arm. Just thinking about it now gives me a facial tic.

That's about when TLC discovered what was billed as World Naked Bike Race Day. Actually, it was two days—March 8 for the Southern Hemisphere and July 14 for the Northern Hemisphere. The idea is to stage an all-nude bike race through some of the world's largest cities to find out who . . . well, to make a statement about . . . uh, to prove . . . what, exactly?

"It's a symbol of how naked bicyclists are in the big city when drivers refuse to share the road," said a poster to the website (www.worldnakedbikeride.org). "We're naked and helpless and invisible. But not on this day."

OK, so it's not exactly a Vietnam protest. But it's something, right? Besides, I'm a bicyclist. When it's nice out, I like to do my errands around town on my bike. Nobody's ever knocked me off my bike or forced me into a ditch, but they've come very close.

I went to the website's FAQ page.

Can I get hurt riding naked on a bike?

Only if you don't wear any sunscreen.

But what about, you know, hurting Coach Johnson?

No, it won't! No hurting or damage will occur if you ride your bike in the normal manner. It will feel just like riding with clothes, but cooler.

But what about hygiene?

Some people fear that they will catch something from the seat or make the seat dirty just by sitting on it naked. Unless you (or your seat) have particularly terrible hygiene already, there won't be a problem . . .

Reassured about my down under from Down Under, we set off.

We were to meet on the midsummer's day of March 8, 2008, at Archibald Fountain in Hyde Park, downtown Sydney, at noon. Not sure how I felt about hearing "bald" and "hide" in regard to my first nude bike race, but there it was.

First thing I did was rent a bike, but when I said to the rental clerk, "So a lot of people renting for the big nude race tomorrow?" he looked at me like bats were flying out of my nostrils.

"Sorry, mate?" he said.

"World Naked Bike Race," I said. "Tomorrow."

"Never heard of it," he said. He seemed to be hanging on to the bike a little longer than I thought he should. Made me feel better, though. At least my bike seat had probably never been in this thing before.

I wondered exactly how a naked bike race would work. Where, for instance, would you pin your number? Where would you put your fiver for emergencies? Would you really want to draft too closely behind another man?

For her part, TLC began to regard the whole affair as a fat-cell convention. She wanted no part of it, a fact that disappointed the organizer to no end once we got to Archibald Fountain. "You sure you don't want to come along?" said Marte Kinder, a tall hippie in a tie-dyed T-shirt and a hat with a plastic sunflower. He had scraggly dreds, a full foodcatcher, and sandals. In other words, exactly the sort of person you'd think would organize the Sydney portion of World Naked Bike Race. "I think you'd *really, really* like it!"

She looked at him like he was Willard Scott offering sexy time. No chance. She'd meet me later.

More troubling, it was beginning to look like Marte and I were the only two going.

"People are staying away because they think we're going to be arrested," Marte confided.

Arrested?

"That's irony, eh? People arrested for being naked right next to statues of naked people!"

"Arrested?" I said, this time out loud. That's about when I noticed the two cops waiting in a squad car about a hundred feet away.

"Well, yeah," Marte hemmed. "They say they're going to arrest us if we do it naked. But they can't arrest us! The law says that indecent exposure must be willful and obscene. So let's say a hurricane comes and whips your pants off; that's neither willful nor obscene. But let's say it rips your pants off and at the time you were masturbating. That's obscene but not willful. But let's say you—yourself—rip them off to masturbate, that's both."

This was starting to be a very bad idea.

Furthermore, Marte pointed out, even if we do get arrested, the T-shirts and the DVDs they sell go toward a fund to defend bicyclists in court. I saw no T-shirt stands or DVD sellers. Instead, I saw myself rotting in a Sydney jail, having monthly meetings with Marte's idiot brother-in-law lawyer, eating vegemite sandwiches three times a day, and fending off the advances of a former roadie from Men At Work.

Besides, Marte says we won't get arrested because the cops don't know where we're going. "While the people will be exposed," Marte said, "the routes will not."

And where ARE we going? I asked.

"We will leave here and reconvene at the University of Sydney," he said. "That's where we'll undress and paint ourselves."

Paint? Reconvene? What the?

It was becoming clear that this was not a race at all. "I wouldn't call it a race," Marte hedged. "I'd call it more gentle exercise." In fact, he said, it wasn't called World Naked Bike Race, it was called World Naked Bike *Ride.*

What was next? *Oh, yeah, and it's not "Naked," it's "Nuked."*

"How far is it to the university?" I asked.

"No idea," Marte said. "I was hoping some other people would show up and lead us."

Wonderful.

But as we waited, people began showing up. Odd, unwashed, sleeping-in-fridge-boxes people. An old, dirty man rode up—his entire life needing a shave—wearing pants that clearly were not originally his. The waist was so big on him that he had to double them over and cinch them with a belt. The fly was permanently down, as was the brim of his bucket hat. He had shoes with no laces in them, and a very stained white shirt. He was either homeless or a flasher. He did not seem like an ardent bicycle-rights activist, if you asked me.

Three guys from Newcastle showed up on bikes, although they were all smoking and looked like they wouldn't make it past the first hill, much less the first cop chase. But at least they had experience with it, unlike Marte or me. They'd done it the year before in Newcastle. "After the race, they had a big party and everybody stood around naked cooking sausage," said one of the three, a bristly man with one eye.

Among the things I'd be willing to do naked, grilling sausages over open flames is not one of them.

Finally, an actually recently-bathed person showed up: a young guy named Luigi, who arrived with a killer body, a painted-on fake handlebar moustache, big black-rimmed spectacles with no glass in them, and, scrawled on his back, cryptically, "Don't Vote for Silvio!"

A very tan, very gay man showed up, without a bike. Said he'd run alongside us. He was followed by a fat man in orange sweats with a ponytail down his back. We still didn't have a single woman.

"Maybe this isn't going to work out?" I asked Marte.

"Sure! Sure it will. We expect more than a hundred people!"

Finally, a Chinese girl arrived with a tie-dyed T-shirt that just barely covered her crotch. It appeared she was wearing no pants. Her face was smothered in half-applied sunblock. She wore shiny patent-leather half-boots. And yet she wasn't as bizarre as the next woman, who rode up on a miniature girl's bike with little colorful plastic spoke riders in the wheels, purple tassels, a banana seat, and wearing a dress that Goodwill would've rejected. "I found it on the dump!" she crowed.

We assumed she meant the bike.

That's when one of the cops climbed sheepishly out of his squad car. He put on his hat and ambled over to us at about one block per hour. He looked like he'd rather be sawing off his own hand than coming over to talk to us. He looked down as he walked, perhaps hoping not to see anything ugly—and it was almost all ugly. When he finally got to us, he said to the one-eyed guy, "Are you organizing this?"

"Organizing what?" the one-eyed guy said, coyly. But then ruined it by rolling over on Marte. "He is," he said, pointing to Our Peerless Leader.

The cop turned to Marte's feet and said to them: "You'll follow all the road rules—"

"Yes, absolutely!" Marte said.

"Stay in single file—"

"Of course!"

And then, almost as an afterthought, he kicked the ground and said, "And no full nudity. You'll get a warning and then you'll be arrested."

Groans and complaints from the group.

"No, no. Absolutely no, uh, genitalia," he said, now staring at his own feet.

The gay guy called out, "Is it against the law?"

"No full nudity," the cop repeated, starting to sneak away.

"But if a woman is riding a bike and she's on the seat, then not everything is showing, is it?" Marte said, putting a very fine point on things.

"No full nudity," the cop kept saying. And he was still saying it as he walked away.

"What about wearing a sock?" Marte hollered.

"What if we're painted?" said the ponytailed guy. "Paint is a cover-up!"

You can imagine the shock on people's faces as we rode through the streets of Sydney, what with a woman on a five-year-old's bike and an old lecherous man who could barely pedal and a gay guy running alongside and Mario from Donkey Kong and a pantsless white-faced Chinese woman. It looked like the Tour de Glands.

After about forty-five minutes and six wrong turns, we eventually got to the university. We pulled over to a grassy spot near a cricket field, at which point Marte started handing out a three-page paper upon which were written suggestions of what people could write on their bodies. Such as:

Less gas, more ass!

Ride a bike! Take a bus! Sell your car!

Indecent exposure to cars!

Then all of them broke out all kinds of body paint, stripped down to complete starkers, and started painting themselves and each other.

"Nice wicket," some guy hollered from the cricket field.

So this was my moment of truth. Was I really going to do this? I took a look around at the group. In the age of cell phone cameras, was I really going to add my nakedness to the Sydney touring company of *Hair*?

Still, a chapter is a chapter. I took off my shirt. Took off my shorts. And I was just about to take off my boxers when I heard, "Police. Can I see some ID?"

My heart became a block of ice. End of the road. I could see the headlines, "Yank in Crank Prank." I turned around to face my executioner and it was just the one-eyed guy. "Ahh, I'm only tuggin' your chain, mate!"

Oh, no you're not, pal. Not now. Not ever.

That's when I decided I'd just ride in my underwear. Does that count? No? Tough.

There seemed to be only one fairly sane man there—one of the three Newscastles, a chiropractor named Michael, who seemed perfectly normal except he wanted me to paint "God Is Love!" on his back. He worked in Idaho for fifteen years and just decided he needed a change in life, so he and his wife and four kids moved across the world to Australia.

Me: Do they think it's funny, you doing the nude bike thing?

Michael: Uh, no. My wife doesn't really much care for it. In fact, I'd say she's kind of anti. It's actually one of the few problems we have in our twenty-four-year marriage.

171

Me: Why doesn't she?

Michael: Because she thinks everybody should stay in their little puritan boxes that the Christian world has pushed everybody inside of.

So much for the whole "we bicyclists are tired of being invisible" *raison d'être.*

His one-eyed buddy had no such moral reasons. He just liked the idea of being nude in public. He painted his front to look like a tree. His chest seemed to be the leaves and they worked their way down to his, well, trunk, which he'd painted lavishly in brown. I mean, he worked that trunk over and over, stretching and pulling it this way and that, the way a barber strops a razor. The thing had more coats of paint than a new Lexus.

One guy had painted a peace symbol on his chest in blue, but he messed it up.

"What's that?" somebody asked.

"That's the peace sign," he said incredulously.

"No, I think that's the Mercedes sign."

Perhaps he was protesting not owning a luxury car.

And that's when the real cops showed up.

"Everybody, get your clothes on," the pudgy one growled. "Right now! You're on private property."

"Private property?" Marte said. "This is a university!"

"Yes," the cop said. "Private property."

A tall, dark, bikinied woman who had joined us at the school said, "But I'm a student here!"

Big mistake.

"You are, huh?" said the cop. She shrank back.

"So we could do this on *public* property?" I tried.

"Well, no. Public OR private property. You can't do it. Indecent exposure, mate!"

This outraged Michael, the chiropractor, so much so that he put an athletic sock over his member and stood brazenly in front of the cop, hands on hips in front of him.

172

"No socks!" the cop insisted. (Surely it was the first time any police officer had uttered the command.) "Put on your underwear."

I was starting to warm to the discussion. I figured this may be as close to a war as I ever got to cover.

"So you're making a distinction between underwear and socks?" I asked.

"Uh, well, yes."

"But why? Don't they both cover the offending part? A sock has more material than, say, a thong, doesn't it?"

The cop looked like he wished he'd gone on to college and not picked this particular line of work.

"No!" he finally said. "Because a sock doesn't cover everything. His bum cheeks are just out there, and nobody wants to see that."

"But if he's riding the bike," I reasoned, "then you're not seeing his bum cheeks, right? Then nothing's exposed!"

The cop started fingering his billy club. His face got red. I took half a step back.

"Look, everybody put your underwear on. Everybody put their underwear on and go right now! Everybody! (Then, pointing at the bikini girl) Except you. You stay."

Uh-oh.

She pretended not to hear and mounted her bike. "Hey!" the cop yelled, but she peeled off. He tried to give chase, but his pudginess kicked in. The closest he got was five feet and then she was off and gone. Victory to the Unclear-of-Purpose Semi-Nude Protesters! It was thrilling! Like *The Great Escape*, only with spokes.

There were twenty-two of us by the time we all were chased off campus and settled in nearby Victoria Park, which was so huge no cops were going to come by no how no way. More stripping, only now there were two newspaper photographers there. I thanked the Lord for my boxers. More painting, too, most noticeably by the tiny-bike girl, who had been very busy. She'd stripped naked and was painting her breasts stoplight red. But this was not the disconcerting part. The disconcerting part was that she seemed to have

Don King trapped under each arm. You don't even want to ask about her shaving skills in the most sensitive portions of her body, which she'd also painted red. Her butt she'd painted black, and on her back Luigi had painted—as asked—"Ride for Pride"!

She turned to Sunscreen Girl and said, "You know, you're wearing rainbow colors. You're gay, right?"

Sunscreen girl: (broken English) "No, no, I just like the rainbow colors. That's OK, yes?"

Tiny-Bike Girl hesitated, then pronounced that it was OK.

Mostly, this seemed like it would be Perverts on Wheels. One guy fashioned his shorts so that they were split down the outside of each leg and split along the crotch, so he could lift them up and flash. His schlong was painted blue. I was guessing he wasn't really that big into biketevism, either.

Creepy Bucket Hat Guy had taken off his pants and nothing else. Was there nobody who was here to protest cars not sharing the road? (Or writing a chapter about it?)

As we finally left for our historic and world-changing ride, I noted that every guy was nude except yours truly. Only one of the three women was nude—Tiny-Bike Girl. Nervously, we rode into Newtown, the college town that goes with the University of Sydney. And there—and there!—we were welcomed like returning astronauts!

Everybody LOVED us! We were riding very near the Imperial Hotel, where the infamous drag-show scene was filmed in the movie *Priscilla, Queen of the Desert*. From every bar and café and head shop we got hoots of approvals, thumbs up, whoops, clapping, whistling, honking, "Way to go!"s. We were a large enough group now that we had our own lane of traffic. Do you know how wonderful that is? Not to have to dodge in and out of cars, not to have to pull precariously close to the parked cars so the moving cars can pass? It was heavenly! I wondered how it felt doing all that naked.

"Does it hurt?" I asked Marte, who was finally smiling.

"Nah, it feels great!"

I couldn't help noticing that Marte was rather well endowed. I'm surprised the thing didn't catch in his chain. He should've been forced to tie it to his calf for safety purposes.

The one-eyed guy came riding up to me, wearing only his sneakers and a hat, and said, "I see now why your Lance Armstrong does so well in the races. He has only one testicle! Much more comfortable!"

"And aerodynamic!" I added.

Conversations You Never Thought You'd Have.

Michael, the chiropractor with the disapproving wife, was hollering all kinds of stuff, none of it having to do with bicycling. "There is no shame in the human body! God loves the human body! Only man brings shame to the human body! The human body is beautiful!" Uh, dude? I think that's a whole different parade.

Most of the attention was paid to Tiny-Bike Girl, naturally, including photographs that would run on the *Sydney Morning Herald* online site, as well as all over the blogosphere.

Me, I was having so much fun, all I could think to holler was: "Don't vote for Silvio!"

I make no judgment whether what we did was right or wrong. I came to realize how invisible I really do feel on a bicycle compared to that day, how small and vulnerable. It was empowering to finally be noticed. On the other hand, I'm not sure we needed to be nude to do it. For instance, we passed by a church just as a family came out of it, all dressed up, a mother, father, a nine-year-old-ish girl and twelve-year-old-ish boy. The parents saw us and their mouths fell open in horror. The little girl looked stunned. But the little boy raised his hands in a touchdown salute. His mom was yelling at him, but he wasn't listening. He was whooping and hollering. I have a picture of that moment and I guess it sums up the whole damn experience—horrifying and hilarious, pointless and important—all at once.

Eventually, we were through Newtown and out in the suburbs and—like a date with Courtney Love—the whole thing just sort of lost its charm. Essentially, we were just twenty-two nudes getting our butts sunburned for the entertainment of Pizza Hut employees and bus benches. Plus with all our evading cops before we could get the thing going, we were already four hours into it and I was already late to meet TLC in Paddington.

So I put my shorts and shirt back on, said my thanks and goodbyes, and peeled off the other way, riding as fast as I could, through the left-hand streets of Sydney, nearly getting killed two or three times. At one point a bread truck turned right in front of me while I was going full speed, causing me to hit my brakes so hard that I nearly flipped over.

"What, you didn't see me, pal?" I hollered.

It took me about ten seconds to see the irony.

Afterwards, I couldn't help checking the success of World Naked Bike Rides around the globe, and every single one of them made Sydney look like an agoraphobics meeting. According to news reports, there were 1,000 in London in the summer of that year, 2,600 in Portland, and over 1,000 in Chicago. I fully expect to see pictures of The Ancient Brit on a Schwinn, naked, in front of Big Ben soon.

Also, just FYI, I am buck freaking starkers as I write this chapter. And no, Mr. Editor, I don't want to hear it's a little short.

12

Jarts

I n this business, I've had to mingle with thugs, con men, and murderers. Had to sink into the underworld of filth and lawlessness. Had to go undercover to write about everything from drug dealers to serial rapists.

But nothing prepared me for the criminal element you're about to meet.

Jarts players.

Now banned in America, a Jart (sometimes known as a lawn dart) was basically a weighted spear for children to play with. They were about a foot of metal, with a pointed steel tip on one end and three plastic fins on the other to increase flight speed and direction. Even the box said, *Outdoor Missile Game!* It's not often you get "missile" and "game" stuck together. Sort of like *Indoor Cat Disposal!*

You'd have to list them at the very top of your Most Hideously Dangerous Toys Ever list, kicking ass over panty-waist dangers like lead paint and asbestos. (Also in my personal top five: 5. Socker Boppers—which were just big—and not very protective—boxing gloves for kids. *Mommy, is my ear still on?*; 4. Fun with Chemistry set; 3. Superballs; and 2. The Hot Wheels Melt Your Own Car set, which enabled youngsters to finally heave hot molten wax at each other!)

The box warned to keep away from the business end of a Jart and to use them only as directed, which meant to throw them, underhanded, ten paces toward a little unmanned plastic hula hoop sitting on the lawn. A Jart inside the hoop was worth two points, a Jart within a Jart's length of the hoop was worth one point, the game to be played and scored like horseshoes. Except only an estimated seven people ever actually played the game of Jarts according to the rules on the box. Everybody else—including me and my nine-year-old friends—thought it was much more fun to heave them as high as possible into the sky and then run like amphetamined rodents in every direction hoping to avoid them coming down on our still-soft skulls. Jarts were also great fun for trying to stick in plywood siding at 70 mph, playing Cannibal and Tourist, and hunting the much-hated squirrel. Sometimes we'd play Russian Soldier, in which one kid would fling the Jart at another, and a third kid—wearing all three sweatshirts—would jump in front of the Jart, hollering, "I'll save you, comrade!" Then again, we went to school only to eat lunch.

Apparently, we weren't the only lint-brained Jartists. Between 1978 and 1986, Jarts caused an estimated 6,100 injuries of every kind—from poked-out eyes to craniums with a sudden and unwanted eighth hole. Four kids died accidentally. One adult died not accidentally. Scott Currier of Huntington Beach, California, was killed when attackers "hog-tied and killed him by throwing lawn darts into his back," according to news accounts.

Definitely not mentioned on the box.

The end for Jarts came in April 1987, when a seven-year-old girl named Michelle Snow of Riverside, California, was playing dolls in the front yard while her nine-year-old brother, Paul, played in the back with his two buddies. One of the kids heaved a Jart that wound up flying across the fence and piercing Michelle's head, killing her three days later. Michelle's father, David, a Hughes Aircraft engineer, devoted himself to getting them banned, and he succeeded. The federal government permanently forbade their sale and manufacture the next year, in 1988.

And since that day, they have disappeared like Soupy Sales.

Except in one place—Piqua, Ohio.

Jeff Balta doesn't really look like an outlaw. I suppose he could be on America's 1,000 Most Wanted, except he'd be easy to catch at the post office, since he's a UPS deliveryman. Balta is a usually law-abiding single man. He does not usually defy congressional bans. It's just that one day, he and his buddy, Shane David, were eighteen and hanging around Shane's house, bored to the bejesus, when Shane's mom finally smiled through clenched teeth and huffed, "Why don't you get the Jarts out of the garage?"

And these guys have played them nonstop ever since. Hey, this is Piqua, which is a suburb of Dayton, which is the home of the Wright Brothers. Can they help it if they like to see things fly?

So Balta and Davis started an underground, secret, and entirely hush-hush yearly Jarts tournament, the de facto World Championship of Jarts.

The Jarts world is just slightly more shadowy than the black market for kidneys. Just getting hold of Balta was like trying to find Bobby Fischer. He didn't answer e-mails for about six months. Then, when TLC convinced him we weren't Elliot Ness, he made one phone call, then dodged us for another three months. Finally, she won his trust and wrangled an invitation for me to play in the 15th annual tournament, as long as we didn't print anybody's address or e-mails. The invitation included this warning:

WARNING: Lawn Jarts have been banned for manufacturing and resale in the United States. The government of the
United States has asked that all Jarts be destroyed. In no
way do we encourage or condone children using Jarts.
Injuries from Lawn Jarts can result in serious injury or
possibly even death. Those who play in this tournament
are aware of the dangers of using Lawn Jarts and choose to
take on the responsibilities associated with this sport.

"Only one person has ever really gotten hurt," Balta insists.
"One guy got hit on the knee. It just sorta stuck there. He kinda
lost a lot of blood. We took him to the hospital and he ended up
fine. We told the ER people he got punctured on a rusty chair."

Really? Only one injury?

"Well, a poodle almost got skewered once. But it was blind. It
just kind of wandered out in the middle of the playing field and a
Jart just barely missed it. I mean, if you pay attention, you'll be
fine. But it's not the kind of thing people bring their kids to."

Really? One knee and almost a poodle? That's it?

"Well, there was a beer cooler once. A Jart went through a Styrofoam cooler and poked a hole in a Miller Lite . . . It helps to
know the Flamingo."

The Flamingo is a move a Jartist does when (a) a Jart is coming
toward his foot and (b) he doesn't want to spill his beer. That's
when you do the Flamingo, which is to simply lift your endan-
gered foot out of the way while keeping everything else still, so you
look like a big, pink tropical bird. Veteran move.

Jeff also told us to BYOB, and to hang around after the tournament because guys play money games at night, under a spotlight
they clamp to the deck. "It's pretty strong, but it still doesn't cover
much of the yard."

OK, so in summation, we're going to be throwing mini-spears
at each other, after drinking all day, at night, for money.

I'm *definitely* bringing my poodle.

On the drive in from Columbus, I wondered what the World Championship of Jarts would be like. Would all the hors d'oeuvres be served at Jart tip? Would it be conducted in a basement, away from prying NORAD cameras? Would it be like a floating crap game, where you have to know the secret phrase?

Man thru tiny doorhole: So?
Me: I'll save you, comrade.
Man: OK.

I noticed that in all the literature and on the T-shirts, there was no catchy slogan for the tournament. Balta said they keep trying to think of a name for it but . . . (warning: Jarts joke coming) . . . nothing's stuck.

May I be of assistance?

Jarts Get Under Your Skin!
Jarts Don't Kill People; People Kill People, Occasionally with
    Jarts
Jarts: Mini-Javelins for Kids!

It was July 7, 2007—7/7/7—when we arrived in the suburban neighborhood of the preppy Shane Davis, thirty-four, Balta's partner in the art of Keeping Killer Toys Alive in America.

There were already about fifty people in Davis' spacious backyard, most of them in their late twenties, early thirties, upper middle class, many of them with no flak jackets. A lot of them have made all fifteen tournaments. One friend came every year until she began working for the FBI. Now she avoids it like al Qaeda meetings.

Davis was so into this whole thing, it was a little scary. "I bought this house just for the yard," Davis beamed. "It's perfect for the tournament!" Well, perfect may be a stretch. He spent about $10,000 bringing in ninety truckloads of dirt to fill in a swamp and taking out a bunch of trees in order to get the perfect lawn to poke holes in.

Upon noticing his wife was listening, he added, "The inside is nice, too."

Everybody playing had to sign the same waiver that came on the invitation, and everybody got a T-shirt with last year's winners' names on it. Turns out a man named Geoff Sharp won it twice. Oh, irony!

Then the pregame festivities began. There was a twelve-foot flag hanging from the porch, and bunting, too. Then two men and two women—all of them in the choir—stood on the porch and sang the national anthem. Because there's nothing quite as patriotic as breaking federal law. At the end of the anthem, there were sounds of jet fighters strafing the place. Wow. Really? But it was just Jeff and his boom box.

Then there was a moment of silence for the troops, although I gotta believe if a soldier was there he'd have said, "Are you people crazy? This shit is dangerous!"

Then, through a big PA system, Jeff started explaining the rules and reciting all the disclaimers, and concluded with: "And remember: 'No practicing!' " which, of course was the biggest lie since, "I thought it was flaxseed oil!" Everybody who was any good had been practicing feverishly. They even have a preseason. In fact, this particular preseason, at a party, Jeff stuck a Jart rather snugly in Shane's foot. "He wasn't watching," Jeff explained. It remained in his foot for a second and took out a pretty nice swath of flesh. Lots of blood, as usual. Trip to the hospital, as usual. Thought it better not to tell the ER people the truth, as usual.

Uh, see, this flamingo jumped him and . . .

Anyway, Jeff ended his speech with: "OK, let's get to work."

Work?

I guess it's possible, since the payout was $300 a person for first,

$200 for second, and $100 for third—plus your name on that T-shirt forever—which meant everybody was giving up their NCAA amateur Jart standing, which meant they were professionals, which meant maybe it was work.

Partners were drawn from a hat, which made absolutely no sense, since two extremely good players could get each other and walk away with it (Shane, for instance, got his father, who is also slightly bat-guano crazy about Jarts) and two players who suck at Jarts worse than Dick Cheney sucks at hunting could get each other (I got a thin, curly-brown-haired woman named Allysa Blankenship who hadn't seemed to ever have thrown a Jart in her life).

"Actually, I played my first game the other night," said Blankenship, thirty-six, who works for a company that makes spoons and reels. That was one more game than I'd ever played. We were screwed. Maybe there's a squirrel-hunting division?

Suddenly, the triple-elimination tournament was on. There were four matches going on at once, four Jarts per match, which meant sixteen Jarts flying pretty much all the time, which made the center of the yard a very good place to aerate your neck. Also, you realized right away, this was the single worst place in the world for wearing open-toed sandals, which is what TLC was wearing. Luckily, she was over by the beer tent, getting hit on by the Steve Garvey–looking character who sang the national anthem and had been hitting on her, nonstop, ever since. The guy had all the lines:

"What'd you think of my vibrato?"

"Really? You used to teach history? Tell me about, I don't know, WOODrow Wilson."

"Is it just the light, or are your eyes *really* that blue?"

So she finally excused herself on the grounds that she had to keep notes on my match for the book and quietly came over and stood about eight feet behind me. If she'd have been there from the beginning she'd have noticed that Alyssa Blankenship is to the World Jarts Championship what Jose Feliciano is to the Indy 500.

Lovely woman, Alyssa Blankenship. Very friendly. Great laugh. But sometime in her life she underwent a coordination bypass operation. She'd begin swinging the Jart forward to throw it and let it go at the bottom of the arc, so that it would fly—no joke— five feet in front of her and then *thwangggg!* into the grass. The next time she would let it go well past the usual release point, so that it would fling straight up in the air and nearly pierce the ball caps of the people in the next game over. Or she would suddenly just haul off and throw it farther than some Ford Explorers go on a gallon of gas.

One of these instances was ten seconds after TLC was taking her quiet position behind me and putting her little digital camera to her face. The next two seconds happened in super slo mo:

Alyssa's very dangerous right arm, suddenly swinging forward like she'd had 100 cc's of Barry Bonds High-Quality Arthritic Rub.

Me watching said Jart fly over my head.

TLC, face buried in camera, snapping photo of the plastic ring on the grass.

Alyssa's eyes getting very big.

Me, suddenly spinning around in horror.

Jart, going *splat,* directly into TLC's ankle.

It seemed like it took a full second before TLC jumped up as though chomped by a snapping turtle. She was quite surprised to find a rather large gash in her ankle and a very big, pointy, heavy red Jart lying at her feet.

Definitely should've Flamingoed.

Alyssa Blankenship covered her mouth in embarrassment as TLC hopped on one foot while holding the other, wincing.

"I . . . am . . . SO . . . sorry!" Alyssa moaned.

Shane and Jeff came over, looking like they'd just swallowed hand grenades. "This is so—weird!" Jeff apologized. "We've almost never had anybody injured, ever!"

"Except for this pre-season," I corrected.

"Well, yeah, except for the pre-season."

Smarmy Anthem Man practically pulled a hammy getting over to see if my girlfriend was going to be OK. "I can take her to the ER right now, if you want," I think he said to me. "That way you can stay in the tournament."

Very caring fellow.

As we bandaged TLC up, I pointed out to Jeff that since TLC wasn't in the competition, she hadn't signed the waiver, which meant she could sue. I looked at Shane's brand-new home and yard and said, "What's your equity in this thing?"

Against all odds, Alyssa the Missa and I won our first-round opponent by defeating a guy who was fairly drunk and a man who'd injured his throwing hand in a fistfight two nights before. Us 1, Alcohol 0.

During the break, Shawn sidled up to me like a KGB agent and asked if I'd like to see "the stash."

The stash?

"Yeah, the stash of Jarts."

Shane said the stash keeps the WCJ alive. He said he's obsessed with finding more, since every year, more Jarts break. (Ankles can really damage a Jart.) Every year, they get harder and harder to find. You can't buy them new, of course. You can't find them in any used sporting goods stores. Even eBay doesn't allow them on their site. Someday, there will be no more. Shane is running Edsel races, collecting Braniff miles, gathering dodo bird feathers. Time is running out.

So how does he get the Jarts? He devotes half his life to it. He has a Google alert ding him every time a box of Jarts shows up on eBay. It usually takes eBay about a day to find out about a new, illegal Jarts item, and then get around to deleting the entry and warning the seller, so Shane has to act fast. He sends the unsuspecting seller an e-mail that reads something like:

Dear Jarts Seller,
    In less than 24 hours eBay is going to cancel your auction, as the selling or buying of Jarts on eBay is banned. But you can call me if you want to sell them. I'll give you $35.
                                            Sincerely,
                                            Shane Davis

Shane's garage was a Jarts museum. It was like going to the Havana Auto Show. He had about thirty sets of Jarts of every make and stripe, just about everything but the original Jarts invented in the 1960s by a dentist named Lawrence Barnett in his barn in Fort Edward, NY.

"This has never been opened," he said, handling a set of black-and-white Jarts like a box of Fabergé eggs. "Someday, this box is going to pay for my kid's education."

To Jartmouth, obviously.

Just then, Shane's wife walked in. "Is he showing you all his dang Jarts again?" she said, rolling her eyes. "My God, they're everywhere! It's so annoying!"

Behind every great man is a wife who would love to give his collection to the Salvation Army.

Anyway, because of all this, Shane has become the Jarts czar of North America. Some people call him Jart Boy. He gets three e-mails a day from people about how to get Jarts, run a Jarts tournament, or get invited to his tournament. "This year, we had a guy from Seattle who wanted to fly in," Jeff told me. "But we only let in our friends. We don't want this thing to get famous."

It was two days before I realized that was a crack at me.

But the question had to be asked: What happens when you finally run out? When you can no longer find any Jarts anywhere in the world? What happens to the tournament then?

Jart Boy took a dramatic pause, looked me square in the eye, and said, gravely, "I guess that's when we start manufacturing them ourselves."

It was a chilling moment. Like being in the room the very first time one housewife looked at the other and said, "Midge, I really think I'm going to rip the Do Not Remove tag off that pillow."

Alyssa the Missa and I immediately lost the next game, 21–10, to two women, one of whom grabbed her crotch to distract me every time I threw. Women, by the way, have never been on the winning team in the fifteen years of Jarts, for no apparent reason. Open-toed sandals, maybe?

While we were being soundly fricasseed by Miss Charm School and her partner, I had time to think about tournaments I hoped La Crotch Grabber would enter next: the Blind Jarts Open, the Parkinson's Sufferers Open, and perhaps the Special Olympics Nighttime Jart-Off.

Just then, a woman showed up with her baby. Everything seemed to stop. People turned and stared at her as though she had a wolverine in her stroller. She had an expression on her face like, "What did I do?!?" Bringing your baby to a Jarts tournament is like bringing Snoop Dogg to a DEA convention.

Then we lost 21–3 to a fat guy and his skinny partner, then to a pair of guys who could've beaten us on crystal meth, which meant we'd lost three times and we were out.

To celebrate, I opened my can of beer with a sharp Jart plunge. Very satisfying.

The final came down to Shane and his dad vs. Shane's brother and a tall athletic guy named Travis, who somehow was no relation to Shane and yet a good Jartist himself. The mood grew tense. In fifteen years, working like a slave on this tournament, scrounging Jarts worldwide for this tournament, buying a *home* just for this tournament, Shane had never won it. So, just before it started, he did a startling thing. He went into the garage and brought out the College Education Jarts.

Epic, dude.

It was the best two out of three to see who would be considered—arguably—the two best Jarts players in America. Sort of like competing to see who were the Two Best Rotary Phone Dialers in America.

In the end, Shane and his dad won and I really thought Shane was going to cry. Everybody was backslapping him and shaking his hand, and then suddenly a wellspring of emotion rose in him and he went into that angry-jubilant-defiant thing that male winners in sports do nowadays where they suddenly seem to be angry, and he started yelling, "This is MY house! This is MY house!"

Actually, Shane, once TLC perfects her limp, it'll be ours.

13

Homeless Soccer

And now, introducing the starting lineup for *your* United States of America World Cup soccer team:

At one forward, a man who slept six months in a graveyard this year, Ray-Ray!

At defenseman, fresh from a bust for cashing stolen checks and possessing a weapon, Pop!

And at goalie, a man who lives on the streets because, as he says, "guys steal from you in the shelters," Reggie Jones!

Did I mention that this is the starting lineup for the United States of America *homeless* soccer team? And they are playing in the *Homeless* World Cup?

Yes, against all logic, the Homeless World Cup actually exists.

This one was scheduled for Copenhagen in August 2007. How could it get any dumber than this? You combine a very dumb sport by itself—soccer—with an even dumber premise, and you're there! The main question I had was: If a homeless team *did* happen to win the Homeless World Cup, where would they put it? In their grocery cart?

The more I thought about a homeless World Cup, the more disgusted I got. This one didn't seem just plain old dumb-as-feet dumb. This one seemed abusively dumb. Of all the things the world's homeless cried out for, I thought, corner kicks did not seem to be one of them.

Dumber still was that forty-eight countries would be competing. Forty-eight countries had nothing better to do than scour their streets looking under wads of old newspapers for soccer players? Exactly how would you identify the best homeless soccer players in your nation, anyway? *Hey, you! Under the bridge! Let's see your bicycle kick!* And how on earth do you schedule practices? There ain't exactly a phone tree, I was guessing.

Then we read there were going to be huge stands set up for the fans. Fans? To watch homeless people play soccer? What exactly was the amazing skill they'd display? Drinking and dribbling at the same time? Was there a large demand to watch guys in mismatched boots take penalty kicks?

You knew there was going to be more sandbagging than the Donald Trump Member-Guest. The rules were vague. Basically, you had to be homeless within the last year, or in rehab, or in asylum. *OK, the bad news: Your house just burned down. The good news? You're starting at forward.*

You could picture the Brazilian coach going, *Uh, this is our striker, Ronaldinho. Many is the night he has spent on the streets. Yes, he was in his limo, but still.*

Mostly, the whole idea just seemed cruel. Seemed like somebody's idea of a yuk at someone else's expense. *Let's watch these bums stumble around and throw up! Be hilarious on YouTube!* How stupid was it to spend 3 million euros flying the world's homeless to a damn soccer tournament when that money could go to, I don't know, homes?

Man, was I wrong.

Usually in Copenhagen, everybody looks like Sting, including the women.

But on this week, everybody looked like Moms Mabley. Dentally speaking, first-grade class pictures have more teeth. This was soccer? The so-called "beautiful game"? There was one catcher's-mitt-faced woman named Isabel—she played for Spain—swear to God, not a single tooth in her head.

That's how you knew, right away, that this whole thing might be real. Because these people really *were* homeless. You could tell by the epidemic boniness and the asphalt-carved skin and the Oakland airport haircuts. These people really had been pulled up from their steam grates and their doorsills and flown to Denmark to play, of all things, soccer. Not just play soccer, but play soccer in the middle of Copenhagen's main square, right in front of City Hall, in two walled soccer pitches the size of a kids' YMCA basketball court, with full stands on each side and game announcers and the Crown Prince of Denmark watching, for the love of Jesus.

And what were they watching? Merely some of the worst soccer known to man. Pitiful dribbling. Clueless passing. Goalies diving for the ball a second and a half after it had come to rest in the back of the net.

The games were two seven-minute halves. Most teams had a few women. No rules on playing them or not. Three players on the pitch plus the goalie. Two could play the whole field, one had to play only on the defensive half. Although, with the field only seventy feet long and the goalies generally having all the athletic skills of grouper, plenty of goals were scored by defensemen just firing from their own end line.

But there were two things homeless players did far better than the pros:

1. Draw fouls. In trying to draw a whistle from the refs, your true World Cup soccer player will get brushed lightly with a kneecap and then fall to the ground and writhe around like he's been pole-axed. When your homeless World Cup soccer player writhes around, it's much more believable, probably because he usually *has* been shot before, and . . .

2. Celebrate. After every game—even if it was 21–0—all the players would gather in the center of the pitch, form a line, grab hands, raise them over their heads with utter joy, and then go rushing up to the crowd with a festive "Heyyyyyy!" Every time, the crowds would give them standing ovations and the players would hug and the referees would hug and the opposing coaches would hug. You'd have thought they'd all just won the European League Championship. Only it wasn't fake or cheesy or over the top. You could just feel what a singular moment it was for homeless people—people that this crowd would usually cross the street to avoid—to be cheered lustily and long and honestly.

Actually, once you met them and heard some of their stories, you damn near wanted to hug them yourself. Like a kid on the Ghana team who became homeless when he lost all his papers while traveling in South Africa. Without ID, he had no way of getting home, getting a job, nothing. So he walked into a mall and stole the first thing he saw—a candy bar—then walked up to the security guard and said, "I stole this." Only they didn't send him home to prison, they sent him home to a mental institution. Which turned out to be a break, because that's how he found the Ghana soccer team.

Or the Australian team captain, goalie Adam Smith, who had enough holes in his eyebrows, nostrils, lips, and ears to easily display the entire jewelry collection of all four Desperate Housewives. Adam usually sleeps in a parking lot. Not in a car. Under a bush. Possibly because he's a schizophrenic. Which might be a rule violation in itself. *Hey, no fair! They've got two guys in goal!*

The other thing I should mention about Adam is that he robs banks.

"See," he explained, "I got a court order to stay on a certain kind of drug. And I *hated* that drug. Just hated it. I appealed and appealed and they wouldn't let me off it. But then I found out that the only way to have the (order) rescinded was to be sentenced to a prison term of two years or more. So I went and robbed a bank. It wasn't much money, really. I was just walking in and robbing one teller. But nobody caught me! So I robbed two more. I really thought I'd gotten away with it. But then, four months later, somebody saw me on *Crimestoppers* and turned me in. I was going into work and I was greeted with the butt of a gun right in my forehead."

Now, you tell me, who else would you want as your captain?

But our favorite player was a young kid on the Zimbabwe team named Faral Mweta, just for the fact that until the moment he checked into the team hotel, he had never slept anywhere with walls, carpeting, or plumbing. Never! In Zimbabwe, Mweta lives under a piece of plastic, though this in itself is an achievement. With inflation at 100,000 percent at tournament time, the sheet of plastic and the poles he needed to hold it up went for one million Zimbabwe dollars. Mweta couldn't afford that, so he had to go out and cut down branches instead. His roof is flat, though, so when it rains, the roof collapses on him. Either way, he sleeps on mud floors. So you can imagine his face when he checked into his fifteenth-floor room in his Copenhagen hotel—a one-star hostel to you, heaven to him.

"Oh, oh, oh!" he beamed when recounting the moment. He threw his head back and laughed, with his huge smile just completely annexing his whole fabulous face. "When you compare it to what I'm used to? Oh! Oh, oh, oh! It's the best! It's amazing! It's awesome! You must understand, I live without electricity and water. Oh! To have a comfortable bed? To wake up and go straight into the bathroom without having to go outside? To simply switch on a light? Oh, it's awesome! I wake up each day and I am SO happy!"

Made me feel bad about bitching to the front desk about our lumpy pillows.

Mweta was so overcome at living this week in first-world style that he refused to delve, even for a moment, into the sorrows of his third-world life. For instance, when I asked him about what made him homeless, he said, "My family, they feel sick and they die."

Your parents?

"They feel sick and then they die."

Your brothers and sisters? "Feel sick, and die."

But what caused them to feel sick and die?

"Sickness is sickness and dead is dead," he said.

Hey, there's no moping in homeless soccer.

This week was the week of wonders for Mweta, who would walk along the streets and stare in disbelief at the shops, the stores, the giant gleaming windows of sparkling treasures. In Zimbabwe, even if he had a penny, there would be nothing for him to buy. "You must understand, all the store shelves are empty. There is no sugar, no bread, no corn, no gas. There are electrical outages all the time. There is no water all the time. Here, they don't run out of water. They don't run out of anything!" As he talked about it, his eyes were saucers and moonbeams were floating out of his mouth. Sigh. "Maybe in another life, I could live like this."

It was that kind of stuff that started melting the ice around my heart toward the Homeless World Cup. I mean, you should've seen the way these people wore their uniforms! They practically burst the chests out of them, they were so proud. In five days, I never saw one of them in street clothes. True, the soccer they played in those uniforms was laughable, aimless, and hopeless, but the way they wore their nation's uniforms you'd have thought they were Manchester United (which, by the way, let the English team train on its pitch).

I went from spitting *Whose ridiculous idea was this?* to rejoicing *Whose wonderful idea was this?*

Turns out it was two editors of a homeless street paper in Scotland called *The Big Issue*—Mel Young and Harold Schmed. One night over beers at a homeless paper convention in Cape Town, the drink led to a think.

What if we tried something different? they said to each other. *What if, instead of trying Way No. 147,383 to try to scrape together enough money for somebody's lunch or somebody's night in a fleabag or somebody's unending prescription, we went at it from the opposite angle? What if we gave them something to be proud of, something to feel good about? What if that thing made them feel better about going out and finding their own lunch and their own housing and their own way off their medication?* So using the hundreds of contacts they had at that convention, they decided to throw a worldwide soccer tournament. Now, *that's* an idea that could never work, right?

"It's been *way* beyond my wildest dreams," says Young, a handsome grayhair of fifty-three. "When we dreamt it up, we only thought we'd have one event. I now do this full time!"

Can you imagine this man's job? Just imagine—for one horrible moment—the task of getting about 500 rootless, drug-and-booze-besotted drifters from around the world into one country for a week. Young slaps his forehead. "The biggest challenge is just getting them visas. Most of these guys don't have passports; some don't even have identities. 'How old are you?' *I don't know.* 'Where were you born?' *No idea.*"

The American coaches—two former Division I soccer-playing brothers from Charlotte, NC, named Lawrence and Rob Cann—will tell you coaching disenfranchised nomads to play the team game of soccer is tiddlywinks compared to getting them on that plane to the tournament. "Do you have any idea how hard it is finding handwritten birth certificates for these guys?" asks Lawrence. Says Robb, "We're getting so good at it, I could get almost any American, born in this country, a passport in one week, start to finish."

Then imagine trying to get it all paid for. The tournament site operations were paid for mostly by the Danish government, with other help from Nike and a few other companies, which probably never dreamed they'd be getting good press out of endorsing crystal-meth addicts and felons.

Just Do It. But Not at Halftime.

The criticism pours under Young's door and over his transom. "We hear it all the time. 'How could you spend all this money for sport? Why not get them housing instead?' I'll tell you why. It doesn't work! There are all kinds of empty houses, but you can't get them to move into them. They are so marginalized. If they're on drugs and alcohol, they're not going. This process—getting them off drugs, giving them some pride, giving them some responsibility, having them be part of a team, something outside themselves that gets them ready to live in a house. Handing them a month's rent, it doesn't work."

When the tournament is over, does it work? Young says 35 percent of the players got a job since the last tournament, 44 percent improved their housing situation, and 92 percent said they had a new motivation for life. "When I first saw those figures, I said, 'That's crap. Not possible.' But we track them. 'What are you doing now? Where are you living?' It's working . . . You know, it costs $60,000 a year for someone to be homeless. Police time, services. They're seventy percent more likely to end up in hospital. No insurance. So if we keep five hundred guys from being homeless—that's five hundred times $60,000—that's, what, $30 million? That's a pretty good investment."

It's possible. For a lot of the players we talked to, just getting on the team changed their lives. If they really wanted to play and be part of it, they had to stop using drugs or they'd be throwing up every day during tryouts.

"A guy might say, 'You know what, I'm not gonna take drugs the night before a game,' " said George Halkias, the Australian coach. " 'It'll spoil the fun.' So they don't!"

Ireland's best player, Trevor Curtis, twenty-six, was a heroin addict. He'd been on the school soccer teams in Dublin as a teenager, but then his mom suddenly died of asthma. "My da's a drinker," Curtis explained. "I've no contact with him." The grief of losing his mom was a black stone in his chest. He began to sink. He got into drugs, was disowned by his family, started robbing to feed his jones, and went to prison for eighteen months. Lucky for him.

"The treatment center was next to the pitch," recalls Curtis. "They were playing five-a-side. So I tried. I was in terrible shape. I couldn't run for ten minutes. Nah, five minutes. Unless I was runnin' from the police, then I could run all day, but for this, nah." In order to make the team, he stopped using. He slept on the streets near the pitch. "Nobody'd rob me. I had nothin' to take." He became Ireland's captain. Now his family—"eight sisters and four brudders"—are back in his life. "They're proud of me now. I ain't out there takin' drugs. I'm playin' for me country. Before it was like I was stuck in the crossroads, y'know? Just everything coming at you this way and that and you don't know which way to go and you know you could die any minute. I don't feel that way no more."

And how does it feel to have people cheering for you?

His face goes 10,000 watts. "Oh, man, I love it! I lap it up! People used to walk around me when I was lyin' on the streets. Now they come right up to me and say, 'Give us a picture?' " Last we checked with him, he was working toward going to college and studying coaching in Dublin. And if his mom could see him now?

"My ma? She'd say, ' 'at's me boy!' "

The Homeless World Cup remains the only sport I've ever covered where everybody on both teams seemed delighted anytime *anybody* scored. Vince Lombardi would've hated it, but I grew to love it. Just to see a man score and raise his arms and see the old needle marks and realize that's a kind of score the guy probably never thought he'd make.

Occasionally, you'd see a player who was three light-years better than the others in wind and skill and savvy—Russia had one—and curl your lip, but Young insisted they weed out the cheats. "You can tell who's really homeless and who isn't," he said. "Homeless people are smart. They know who's a fraud. They'll quiz them. 'Do you know this soup kitchen? No?' They start to get suspicious rather quickly."

Except the Afghanistan team, of course. According to their coach and *chef de mission*, Raz Dalili, there *are* no homeless in Afghanistan. He said it like there was a man standing next to him with pruning shears, waiting to chop his tongue off at the first ill-chosen word, but he said it.

> Dalili: There are no homeless in Afghanistan. They stay
>   with family. The families take them in.
> Me: Really? No drug users living on the streets?
> Dalili: No, there is no drug abuse in Afghanistan. We have
>   none of that.
> Me: No homeless from the Thirty Years War, or the Taliban
>   takeover, or the American invasion?
> Dalili: Yes, 2.5 million people from the war, but the families
>   took them all in. Life is better now, but hopelessness is
>   bad again, like four years ago, it's bad again.
> Me: So, utter hopelessness, but no homelessness?
> Dalili: No.
> Me: Think any of your players will seek asylum here?
> Dalili: No, why would they?
> Me: Hopelessness?
> Dalili: No. And if they did, I would turn them into the
>   police. Besides, these players, they will be better off. They
>   become famous for being on this team. They get jobs. We
>   pay them $80 a month.
> Me: I noticed your players don't congratulate your
>   opponents after games.
> Dalili: It is bad luck; they are enemies of Afghanistan.

Who knew Afghanistan was so hard up for enemies?

Mostly, though, it was a week in the life of about 500 homeless people like none they'd ever spent. They were suddenly transferred from "diseased pariah" to "esteemed star." That took some getting used to. For instance: On the cover of the tournament program—which was everywhere—there was a Denmark player with a world-class Afro and bottomless brown eyes. He had suddenly gone from a bum sleeping on a ripped oven box to a local hero. "I am famous now," he said. "People are asking me for autographs. It's crazy. It's like a blessing." As he talked, I noticed that all his homeless drunk friends were waiting for him, with bottles of wine in paper bags and filthy coats and the aroma of unbathed lemurs. They kept yelling things at him in Danish that sounded like, "Party with us, dude! Have a drink! Give us a cigarette!" He'd look back at them and then look at me and try to finish the interview, but it was making him a little uncomfortable. "They are happy for me," he said, swallowing. "But they, they—well—they—"

Got it.

The American team, for instance, had a documentary film crew following them everywhere they went. Which was kind of different for guys the Chamber of Commerce tries to sweep off the streets before they take postcard pictures. Most of them were from Charlotte—where the Cann brothers run an urban ministry center—despite holding tryouts in other American cities, like Philly, New York, Atlanta, and Austin.

They managed to find some not entirely awful players, though. The fastest was a twenty-four-year-old from Honduras named Daniel Martinez, whose family moved to New York City when he was a boy and whose father died shortly thereafter. "He got sick and he died," Martinez explained. Yeah, lot of that going around.

They found their starting goaltender, Reggie Jones, with a big swollen black eye on the day of his tryout. He'd won a little job in a warehouse and got jumped for his trouble. The team was driving back into Charlotte after a tournament in DC, and Rob said, "OK, now where does everybody need to go?" When they'd dropped off everybody, they looked back and found Reggie still sitting in the last row of the van. Awkward pause. "We just sort of dropped him off at the center . . . and he just sort of disappeared into the night," Lawrence remembers. Turns out he was a refugee from Sierra Leone who left there with his mother in 1996. But she met a man and threw him out—in no particular order—and he's been on his own ever since.

"I love waking up in the morning and having something to do," he said. "I wake up happy. I go to the center, and I do art, and then I play soccer. I like being on a team. I don't want to disappoint the other guys. I don't want to let them down. Now, if somebody gives me a loaf of bread, I break it in half and give it to somebody else."

And at night?

"At night, if I have a little money, I can go to a friend's house and say, 'I have $20. Can I spend the night here?' Sometimes it's yes and sometimes it's no. So then I walk the streets all night. I can't lie down and sleep or they steal my clothes. They steal my shoes. Sometimes I get too sleepy and I find an open spot—a big open spot—and I stay on the open side, where people can see me and I can see them."

You think David Beckham has that problem?

Coach: You suck today, Beckham! What's your problem?
Beckham: Well, I walked around town all night, Coach.
*   Couldn't find a big open spot that was safe enough.*

The USA's best player was a guy who really *had* been shot—Dave McGregor—and not shot like Barry Bonds or Roger Clemens, syringe-shot. Shot shot. The whole team was a kind of Bad News Bears in real life. One player, Ray-Ray, had his house burned down, leaving him without a roof and without a hope. He started sleeping in the graveyard because, he says, "people are superstitious and won't go in there at night." He's started to make a life comeback playing on the team. He's been selling some of his paintings and he's got his own place now. Good thing. He has eight kids.

Now they were wearing *USA* across their chests and suddenly doing things they'd never dreamed. For instance, the American ambassador to Denmark showed up on Day Three, noticed the documentary crew, and suddenly wanted to give the team an inspirational speech, a few hugs, and maybe a few photo ops. Suddenly, Pops—who'd been in jail not long before—was getting asked by an ambassador if he could take a photo with him.

Wonder if, out of habit, Pops had to swallow the urge to take it from the front *and* the side?

Not that it matters, but the winner of the whole Homeless World Cup was Scotland, which beat Poland in the final 9–3. The Americans finished in the bottom half, going 1–2 in the opening rounds—losing one game to Burundi, 4–2, though that's no shame, since Burundi has a mess of homeless people. In their final game, the Yanks lost to Greece, 7–6, in a battle for—as the publicity release said before the game—"the honor of being named the 33th best team in this championship." What do you get for "33th"? Something made of aluminum?

Faral Mweta's Zimbabwe team finished in the bottom half, which was nothing compared to the sorrow he must've felt turning in the key to his beloved hostel room. Adam Smith, our schizophrenic Aussie bank robber, captained the team that played nearly the worst but had the most laughs. Scotland beat them in one game 13–0. "True," Smith allowed, "but we held them to less than a goal a minute!" Their greatest victory probably came from a typo. The tournament secretary typed "Australia" for a consolation trophy game when she meant to type "Austria." So both Australia and Austria showed up, and it took them about ten minutes to figure out that it was really Austria that should be playing, which was a good thing, because Austria got cleaned like Aretha Franklin's fork, while Australia got to watch.

But this was the topper: Remember that Spanish woman with no teeth? Isabel? She actually scored a goal. True, it was phonier than Velveeta, but it was a goal. Spain was getting whupped by Ireland 10–1 with a minute left when the Spanish coach finally put her on the pitch and Ireland decided to play along and let her kick one and the goalie pretended to fall down just short of it and it rolled like an anesthetized sloth into the net.

It took her a full second to realize what she had done and then she went absolutely bananas. Her teammates picked her up and carried her aloft while the Irish players cheered her from below and then even some of *them* carried her for a while. Her head flopped backwards and joy flowed out of her toes and ears. It had to be, far and away, the greatest moment of her life, and you knew it because her block-wide smile showed every single one of her missing teeth.

Hmmm. Maybe it really IS a beautiful game.

Conclusion: The Winner

The best TV show ever is *Andy Griffith,* partly because at the end, Andy would strum his guitar on the front porch and wait until it suddenly hit six-year-old Opie what the lesson of the week was, usually something like, "Maybe I shouldn't have burned down the silo."

So what lessons did we learn in trampling the globe to find the world's dumbest sport? Well, for one, we learned how to make our projectile vomits extremely colorful and sticky. You know, if we're asked to perform at bar mitzvahs. For two, if you must put large hairless rodents down your pants, it's better to remove all penile jewelry. And three, very few black people are into this country's underground Jarts movement.

The dumbest sport in the world? Besides baseball? It's gotta be chess boxing. I'm sorry, but I just couldn't help but laugh every time I'd see some poor geek get the cobwebs wopped out of him by a right hand one minute, then have to play the Sicilian Defense the next, blood dripping from his nose, eyes crossed. That's just dumber than a wheelbarrow of toupees.

But what surprised me the most was just how *not* dumb a lot of all this was. What I learned more than anything is that the number of people who watch a sport or play a sport or have ever heard of a sport has zero to do with how much guts or passion or skill the people who play it have.

I've covered great athletes for thirty-plus years, but I'm not sure any of them could do what Edward (ET) Trotter could do. Remember? He was the Angola State Penitentiary prisoner who lets 2,000-pound bulls run *over* him so that he can reach up as he's being trampled to pull off a $500 chip. I mean, honestly, were he in the same position, would LeBron James do that?

Or Desiree (Dez) Weimann, the little mortician's-assistant running back. She's got to be in the top three women in America at what she does, and yet she pays for her own equipment, pays for her own travel, and works a full-time job just to keep playing. Has Adrian Peterson ever had to do that?

And I can't get out of my mind Leila Kulin, the woman with a face like an Easter Island statue who sat in that 261-degree sauna in Finland as though it were a park bench in Central Park. While the woman next to her was going into triple fits, she sat there and didn't move so much as a cuticle. Her skin was literally frying and yet she didn't even blink. Has Tiger Woods ever been more focused?

My Opie moment was this: Turns out "dumb" is in the eye of the beholder. You couldn't see the face of one of those homeless soccer players as he soaked in a standing ovation and think it was anything but pure grace. Really, considering my preconceived notions of what these sports would be like vs. what most of them actually were like, maybe I was the dumbest of all.

Still, I did do one smart thing during this quest. About two and a half years into it, I married TLC. I love her. She loves me. And for lonely nights, she beats the bejesus out of ferrets.